Woman to Woman

Conversations with Mary

Jeannette M. Cooper

AVE MARIA PRESS NOTRE DAME, INDIANA 46556

© 1988 by Ave Maria Press, Notre Dame, Indiana 46556

Library of Congress Catalog Card Number: 88-71021

International Standard Book Number: 0-87793-383-9

Cover photograph by Robert Maust

Cover and text design: Katherine A. Coleman

Printed and bound in the United States of America.   .

Dedication
To my mother and to Mom C.
With grateful acknowledgment to "the listeners"
and to Sam.

Contents

Introduction:
Letters to Mary

One evening, while some friends and I were dining, the conversation turned to Mary, Blessed Mother. "Whatever happened to her?" someone asked. "You just never hear much about her anymore," another declared. "She was so much a part of our religion," someone else added. And so it began. As the discussion progressed, each of us had something to contribute in the way of memory but, with the exception of a couple of men present, none of us had maintained any particular devotion to her. In fact, few of us could even remember the last time we had prayed the rosary. "Probably at a funeral!" one of the women noted. We all laughed in assent.

The conversation wended its way into other topics but I was intrigued by the talk about Mary and remembered it a few weeks later when, meeting with the editors of the San Diego Cursillo paper, I was asked to write a column for it. "May I write about anything I want to?" I asked. "Yes," I was told. "About Mary?" I asked. "Sure," came the reply. "Why not? The Cursillo Movement is dedicated to her though nobody ever really talks about it. Do whatever you want."

After trying several approaches to the column, I finally settled on a letter format. I felt this gave me a starting point for each column and it allowed for an immediacy and intimacy that an essay form did not. We labored over a name for the column and finally fell back on the obvious "Letters to Mary."

The response was good and as the columns continued to appear, positive comments kept coming in to both the editors and myself. As I listened to those comments I came to realize that in my letters I was not proposing something novel. Rather, I was simply articulating what hundreds in the community had been feeling but not expressing—the Mary of our youth was lovely but not real to us.

She had been so mythologized that we had lost her. She had become a mystery rather than an essential part of the mysterium. We need the woman, not the titles. We need, as St. Therese of Lisieux said, "a sermon on the Blessed Virgin [which would] show her real life, which the gospel gives us hints about, and not an imaginary life . . . We can well guess that her real life, in Nazareth and later, must have been very ordinary." We need her to come alive for us, to come in and sit at the kitchen table, to share her humanity so that we can, in turn, share ours with her.

I hope these conversations with Mary will awaken in us a renewed sense of Mary as woman—human, real, ordinary, alive.

Hello Again, Mary

I have so much I want to tell you, Mary, so much catching up to do. After all, it has been years since we really talked. A lot of changes have taken place since then, changes in me and in my life; changes in my perceptions, in the ways I view things . . . people . . . and you.

I've grown up, Mary. The young women who were yesterday's little girls in my neighborhood are now married with children of their own. I want a relationship with you as they do with me.

I want a relationship that isn't based on petitions alone (''Please let them buy my girl scout cookies so I can win the prize'') or personal problems (''Please make him call me tonight . . . I'll just die if he doesn't call me''). I have no petitions, no entreaties, no need to beg favors of you. I have only a heartfelt desire to know you, to explore a real relationship with you, to become friends.

I hope you do not mind that I address you by name.

I simply cannot bring myself to call you Blessed Mother as I did when I was a child. I would feel as young and naive as I did then.

You are the patroness of the Cursillo Movement, but that's not something I can call you. I wasn't even particularly moved by learning that, soon after I made my Weekend. I certainly wasn't surprised. You have so many titles. What was one more?

Rose of Sharon and Lily of the Valley are just a little much, don't you think? I mean, nice if addressed to you by some troubadour or knight in shining armor on Valentine's Day. But by another woman who has been through the mill and back again? Really!

One day, while walking in a garden near a shrine dedicated to you, a thought as light as the caress of a wind-blown leaf brushed my mind. I wondered about the woman hidden behind all those titles, the person all but buried underneath countless dedications of everything from small poems to huge concertos to whole countries, not to mention chapels and churches and cathedrals.

I thought back to my childhood images of you. You were my blessed mother, young and slim and beautiful. You stood serene, with never a frown or wrinkle. And you had the loveliest hands.

I called you mother and yet, when I look back, you were more for bringing flowers to and weaving garlands for. It was to my own mother that I took my grubby things, my grubby self. Her hands were not nearly so lovely as yours. Somehow, you always got my Sunday best.

I suppose, though, that little girls have a need for someone to arrange flowers for, for someone to bring no-strings-attached gifts to. Forgive me for wishing I had woven more garlands for my own mother and shared with you a little more of my grubbiness. It might have saved us all some grief. In my little girl's eyes you were perfect. How could any earthly mother ever live up to you?

Somehow, I never thought of you as a little girl. I knew you had a mother, Anne, but I never related to you as anything but Blessed Mother. I wanted to grow up and be just like you: beautiful, slim, ever-young. I wanted to be as unspoiled and pure, as serene and lovely as you were.

You were so special to me then and I hold those memories warmly. I mentioned titles. But I remember the litanies. How they rolled off the tongue and rose like bright colored balloons to you. I had my favorites. Just hearing them was an enchantment to me.

But I grew older, Mary, and somehow you seemed not to. You became less "mother" and more "virgin," purest of the pure. There was a period in my young womanhood when I still tried to emulate you. But it became more and more difficult, until one day, married, knee-deep in wall-to-wall children, frustrated, exhausted, I turned from you. So deep was my disillusionment that I lettered a sign and pinned it to the refrigerator: "It's easy to be a perfect mother if you have a perfect Son and only one of them at that!"

After that, I seldom spoke to you, and then only to make polite conversation. I nodded in passing and continued to wend my way round the rosary. But something had died in me.

It took these many years for me to understand that "something" had little to do with you. It is a measure of my maturing that I accept your understanding of what I am telling you about those early years. I do not think that you have changed, Mary, but I have.

One of Those Days

Did you ever have one of those days? Joseph was up early and off to get measurements for someone's cabinetry. You called Jesus to get up for classes with the local rabbi. And called. And called.

He's finally breakfasted and off, and you put the dishes to soak, start to gather the laundry for the trek down to the river, when you hear a call followed by the entry of the woman up the alley who comes in and plops herself down to discuss the latest wrinkle in the Roman occupation. It's an old topic and you've heard it all before and you know she'll get to the real reason for her visit: Her son has joined a band of zealots and gone off to Bethany near Jerusalem and she's worried.

An hour and a half later she has exhausted her concerns and gone (Praise Yahweh!) and you're wondering if there's a decent spot left on the river bank when a child comes, sent by the rabbi, to inquire why Jesus hasn't come to class yet.

You throw on a shawl and after a few false leads

find him skipping stones across the water downstream. You speak softly while walking him to the rabbi's class but somewhere in the recesses of your mind you feel a faint gathering of storm clouds. Consciously you begin to breathe a bit more deeply.

You get back home only to find the family goat loose and in the house getting ready to feast on one of Jesus' Sabbath Day sandals. The storm surfaces and with it a burst of energy that saves the sandal, chases the goat out to its pen, sweeps up the broken crockery and sets the house somewhat to rights.

The day's half over, the laundry's not done, Joseph isn't home and experience tells you that things will probably get no better until the next rising of the sun.

What did you do then, Mary? Utter an unspeakable word? Volubly paint a local curse with your own colors and include in it not only this day but yesterday with its bill collector, its outrageous price for chicken and Jesus using your best sash (your only sash) to harness the donkey?

Did you realize, in the tears tracing your cheeks, that the storm has spent itself and there will be none left over for Jesus and Joseph when they return home?

Too late now to do the laundry, so you gather the vegetables for supper and sit, your hands automatically stringing and peeling while your mind, in that slow motion way it has of reconstructing the past, takes you back to Gabriel. It all started with Gabriel.

An ordinary day, that one, broken by an extraordinary visitor. Once again you feel yourself in the presence of the angel, not with fear and trembling but with that sense of recognition the soul possesses in meeting its own. You feel an instant authenticity more real than that felt in human relationships that generally need time to develop.

Gabriel appears outside of time and you trust him

with no explanations required. He greets you and says "The Lord is with you." You are puzzled, wondering what he means. Then he tells you that you have "won God's favor . . . you are to conceive and bear a son . . . you must name him Jesus." Gabriel goes on, further identifying this child you have been chosen to carry within your womb.

But you are an intelligent young woman, and a practical one. You know the manner in which a child is conceived, the customs of your people regarding marriage and children. You are secure in your knowledge and just because an angel says you are to conceive a special child you suspend neither your intelligence nor your knowledge. You are not coy about the mysteries of life, so you ask, "But how can this come about, since I am a virgin?" Gabriel replies: "The Holy Spirit will come upon you and the power of the Most High will cover you with its shadow. And so the child will be holy and will be called Son of God."

Right then and there, Mary, you made a decision. You said: "Let what you have said be done to me." You felt no need to consult anyone about that decision. So secure were you in your relationship with God that you could say yes without seeking counsel from your rabbi, your father, anyone. Even in a patriarchal society your sense of self-worth was so genuine, your communication with God so real and so direct that you questioned his own messenger, evaluated his words and then, without any protestations of unworthiness, you stated your amen, your "so be it."

To a generation of women, conditioned from childhood to equate spirituality with docility and unquestioning obedience, your conversation with Gabriel is a remarkable record of a woman whose spirit could not possibly fit the romantic, pietistic image that some of the early church fathers and later troubadours idealized

you into. In projecting their image of the Virgin Queen
they exalted you into something less than human; perhaps they did not realize that only in the fully human
could the divine be fully nourished.

I visualize you now, sitting with the finished vegetables in your lap, a slight smile on your face, a glow
about your entire being. Re-living Gabriel's visit as-
sures you that what was, is. The love that shaped your
decision feeds upon its recollected self, fills you,
streams from you, bypassing time, to warm the heart of
one who has had one of those days also.

Seeking Sanctuary

A vermillion sun nestles in the bosom of the hills across the valley as if reluctant to rise and get on with the day. I, too, am reluctant to enter into the heat that the later morning will bring. My daughter will inform me of her decision today, and my niece will arrive seeking sanctuary of a sort.

I bathe my mind in the quietude of these first moments of morning and recall the conversation initiated by my daughter last week. Her thinking of moving out with a boyfriend led to our sharing thoughts on the meaning of love, commitment, sexual intimacy, friendship, choice, consequences. We left the burden of decision upon her shoulders.

Two days ago my niece called and asked if she could stay with us for awhile. Only a year older than my daughter, she's pregnant, father unknown. The harshness of her family's attitude is more than she can cope with right now.

I have walked these past days in wordless prayer,

wondering what to do, what to say. I have thought often of you, Mary, and of your mother. How did you tell
her? When? What did you say? And how did she react?

Gabriel had told you that your cousin, Elizabeth,
well along in age and barren all these years, was with
child. Did you, like my niece, decide that the environment in your neighborhood was too harsh to cope with?
Did you, one dawn, leave Nazareth to go to Elizabeth,
hoping for acceptance, for understanding, for a shared
experience?

Matthew tells us that Joseph wanted to divorce you
informally. The two of you were betrothed. In your culture, betrothal was a serious relationship, tantamount
to marriage. Suddenly, you are pregnant. Joseph is not
the father of your child and the laws of your people are
explicit about such things. Joseph has grounds for public divorce. He does not wish to raise a child not his
own.

Yet the fact that he wants the divorce to be informal,
that is without public judgment and written decree, in-
dicates that he doesn't want to punish you. Too, he
may be mystified at the account you have given him of
the conception. While not understanding, he nevertheless accepts that there is something here out of the ordinary, and so is inclined to leave you free to deal with it.

At any rate, you do walk to Elizabeth's. As far as we
know you go alone, walking the dusty roads of your village with a growing sense of relief. At last you are free
of questions you cannot answer, of anxieties and ten-
sions in the faces around you, free to be alone with your
seedling child, your son to be named Jesus. Whatever
fears you may have had about brigands and thieves
evaporate in the immediacy of your joy at being chosen
to carry the Lord of your people. Outside the village
you choose the road that will lead you to Ain Karim,
near Jerusalem, where Elizabeth and her husband, Ze-

chariah, live. It is a long journey and you hurry along toward the hill country, keeping to yourself, humming quietly, occasionally nodding to those along the way who smile in response to the radiance they glimpse in your eyes.

Only once do you falter. It is hot and you have sought rest from the afternoon sun in the mouth of a small cave. Nibbling some goat cheese, you look around at the deserted and desolate landscape and something of it seeps into you and momentarily you wonder what is to become of you. What if Elizabeth doesn't want you? Where will you find another man as good as Joseph? Who will protect you . . . and your special baby?

The countryside shimmers through your unshed tears. Then you shake your head stubbornly. Yahweh does not desert his own. You repeat the words of Gabriel, and feel foolish. Somehow you know that everything will be taken care of. You rise and start up another hill.

Finally, hot and dirty and sweaty, you arrive at Elizabeth's. Before you have crossed the tiny courtyard the door opens and Elizabeth appears, arms open, gathering you to herself. In that moment you know the arms of Yahweh around you and your tears are released. The two of you embrace while Elizabeth welcomes and comforts you. Suddenly Elizabeth drops one of her hands to her belly, cries out, and before you can react, she acknowledges the fruit of your womb and expresses joyous surprise that the ''mother of my Lord'' should visit her.

Luke has you respond with the magnificat. Though probably not what you actually said, it's an appropriate response. Your cousin has not only welcomed you, but has entered into your extraordinary God-experience in the deepest and most profound manner, with certain

knowledge. As you bathe away the grime of your journey, you must feel an incredible rightness and peace
about your decision to accept the will of Yahweh within
your womb, no matter the consequences.

Ah Mary, two hours have passed. I have lost the
thread of what I was saying. In the meantime, though,
my daughter has informed me that she told her boyfriend no, she will remain at home. My niece arrived,
her mother with her. After talking together, my sister
has calmed down, hugged her daughter (who may be
returning home this very day) and we now are all going
to breakfast.

I sing my own magnificat.

Birth at Midnight

The morning mail brought a box of unsolicited Christmas cards. Three of them show you sitting demurely, sidesaddle, hands folded in your lap, on a donkey led by Joseph. One dainty sandalled foot dangles beneath the folds of your cloak. The two of you are alone and apparently within sight of Bethlehem.

The other three cards have you kneeling, slightly bent forward, arms crossed over your chest, head bowed in adoration of your newly-born son. Joseph stands on the other side of the baby, his face expressionless. Both scenes are common enough artistic renderings, pale prints of accepted classic paintings.

All day I felt a vague irritation and, this evening, picking up those cards, I suddenly caught its focus. Here you are, the enfleshed, human mother of my Lord, riding an unsaddled donkey without even holding on to it in some manner. And you are nine months pregnant! I wouldn't have made it once around a merry-go-round at that stage.

Where is the swollen belly, the swollen feet? How could you sit a donkey like that, with your center of gravity displaced by the child readying himself to enter our world. Where in this painting and thousands of others is the Mary who talked back to an angel, who had the strength of character to make commitments, the courage to go miles alone, the pride to walk with head high, making neither apology nor defense for her choice of life? Surely not in this girl-child whose very body posturing proclaims her a timid, submissive maiden!

And later, in the stable, Mary, what really happened? Certainly not an instantaneous birth sans blood and amniotic fluids, no matter what the early church fathers might have argued. The whole idea was for Jesus to be born of woman, to be born human, to enter into our finite condition so that we could enter into his infinite one. The birthing experience must have physiologically paralleled that of every woman since time began.

I often wonder how that narrative might have read if it had been recorded by a female.

I imagine you arriving at an inn, tired, exhausted, with aching back and signaling contractions. Joseph, too, is weary beyond belief and deeply concerned about you. But there is no room here for you, and no way you can continue down the road. Offered refuge in a stable you murmur: "Fine, Joseph. Take it. I'll be fine. Just fine." Realizing he has little choice Joseph agrees to the arrangement and the two of you go to the stable. While Joseph tends the donkey, you set out your few possessions, including the swaddling clothes for the baby that you now know will be born this night. You gather some clean hay into a bed of sorts, cover it, and gratefully ease yourself down onto it. When Joseph comes in, you send him to the inn to eat some supper, assuring him that you are not hungry. He goes and you rest, gather-

ing prayerful strength for what is to come. Suddenly a
soft voice greets you and you look up to see a middle-
aged woman and a girl. She introduces herself as Miriam and tells you she has been talking to Joseph and
has come to help.

"Now don't you worry . . . this isn't the first babe
I've helped to come into the world . . . now Sarah (to the
girl) run back and get that pot of hot water and don't
forget the rags, the clean ones on the table in the corner.
And wake up Rachel and tell her to come back with
you."

She approaches and sits down beside you, caressing you with her soft chatter. You don't protest her
ministrations for you know that, in the way of your people, she has come to do for you what, in your culture,
only another woman can.

The two younger women return with water, linen
and rags, and the three of them gently prepare you for
the birth. You share, all of you, a little of yourselves until finally, you enter the last stage of labor. Through a
haze of pain you sense rather than feel their working for
you and with you. Suddenly, it's over, and a new cry is
heard throughout the land. Emmanuel, the promise of
ages, is laid naked and crying upon your abdomen.
Flesh of your flesh, God made man, the child is born.
And you exult.

Miriam cuts and ties the umbilical cord, cleans the
baby, wraps him in the swaddling clothes, and lays him
in your arms. After the women have taken care of the
afterbirth and cleansed you, tidied the area, brought in
fresh hay, they kneel reverently to the miracle of new
life noisily learning to suckle at your breast. Then, gathering their pots and soiled rags, they leave you, promis-
ing to send Joseph back.

Ordinarily, Joseph would not have returned to you
for seven days but these were not ordinary times or cir-

cumstances. Bethlehem was bursting at the seams because of the census and there were no women to do
more for you than what had already been done. So Joseph returns to remain with you in your deepest moment of magnificat. And ours, too, Mary. For discovering you behind all the stylized and romanticized art of
the centuries gifts us with dignity, courage and the
power of decision and commitment.

A Screaming Swirling Silence

It's been a while since I last spoke to you. Several times I tried but no matter how I arranged them, my words refused to dance, or even smile, but drooped and fell back into the depression from whence they came.

Were you ever depressed, Mary? Caught in that in-between place where day and night blend into a wash of gray and neither sun nor moon, stars nor sea, child nor friend adds one iota of tone or texture? It is a weariness of soul, a loneliness of spirit so profound that life and death blur and cataclysmic events affect us little more than a child's spilled milk.

Did you ever feel as if the whole world had somehow left you behind in a hollow, windswept place where only the echo of your own voice sounded? And slowly, in that cold space within yourself, even that began to fade until only a screaming, swirling silence remained, a silence that sleep alone could mute.

Much has been said about the astonishing reality of God having chosen you, a woman, an ordinary human,

to be the mother of his son. This is always qualified by
the statement that you were completely ''without sin,''
a qualification, incidentally, which seemed to place you
far beyond the sphere of a woman like me. Now, I wonder if it really does.

I think, in my child's mind, I equated sin with being
human, with being ordinary, so that I had you gliding
(never walking or, heaven forbid, trudging) through
life, hands serenely folded when they weren't holding
your self-composed baby. You never sweated or had to
brush away a biting fly; ants paused to bow at your door
before passing on to enter your neighbor's house. In
short I conjured you up as a kind of heavenly Barbie
doll. A natural result, I suppose, of the romantic and
Victorian images of you in art and spiritual literature.

We are told that you fled Bethlehem by night to avoid
Herod's murderous wrath. Your destination was Egypt, a
country wherein you would have safe passage and refuge. To get there you had to endure sun, wind and dust
as you walked up and down barren hills and crossed the
low desert country to reach the Mediterranean coast,
along which you possibly traveled until you were finally
able to cross over into Upper Egypt. Once there, you
probably sought a refugee settlement of Jews, who, like
yourselves, had fled reprisals in their home country.
Somewhere along the upper Nile, perhaps, they had
carved out a small community into which you settled with
little fuss and picked up the rhythm of life in exile.

In Egypt, if it isn't the sand, it's the floods or the
bugs. The people there are kindly but their gods are
many and strange. Joseph is busy trying to eke out a living for you all. Sabbath is observed by your community
but there is no synagogue, no real rabbi. The women
are helpful, even friendly, but you begin to feel iso-
lated. It takes more and more effort to complete the

daily chores. Some days it seems impossible even to get up in the morning. Things seem to matter less and less but you force yourself to go through the motions. And the tears well up and slide down your cheeks into the soup or onto the garment you're mending. You feel that if you could only sob them out for an hour they would be gone. But you can't. You pray. You beg Yahweh to release you from this prison of yourself. But he seems to have gone away, and you are too tired, bone-tired and soul-tired, to continue calling his name.

Then, one morning, you awaken and stretch into the warmth of dawn. You get up, dress, and hear clearly the song of a bird. You make the tea, taste it and marvel at its robust flavor. You go to the door and are startled by the pungent scent of the marsh grasses growing near the river. You turn to see Joseph and Jesus getting up and you stare for a moment because it is as if they have taken on new dimensions and are somehow larger, more than they were. You hurry to make their breakfast and get them off to their day's activities, giving them each an extra hug as they leave. Throughout the day you clean and wash and scrub, shake out the bedding and hear yourself singing praises to Yahweh while, with your entire being, you eagerly look forward to tomorrow.

I feel better, Mary. Talking about depressions with you, sensing that they were as normal a part of your maturing as they have been of mine, has made me realize how truly we are sisters, women with shared experiences. Trying to understand you as an ordinary human person helps me to accept myself as human and to place emotional depressions into human perspective. In depression we shut down our senses, close out the familiar world to enter into a kind of interior exile. There we wrestle with angels, pose unanswerable questions and painfully ponder the convolutions of life. Depression is a time of dissolving the very fiber of ourselves into that screaming silence, of exhausting our egos so that God can bring us to the stillpoint of himself. There's no sin, no testing, no trial by misfortune about it. Simply a necessary process by which we absorb the strength and wisdom to become, slowly and gradually, fully human.

About His Father's Business

It is almost dawn. Too late to go to bed, too early to face the day. Especially a day in which I must confront my son and set the boundaries of his living here—yet again!

He went to a movie last night with some friends. After the movie, they went to get something to eat. After that, they ended up at one of the friends' houses where, according to him, they talked for several hours. I learned all of this when he crept in, shoes in hand, at 3:22 this morning. He was supposed to have been home by midnight. And yes, I was watching the clock. By one, I was worried. By two, I was frantic. By three, I was furious. Not even a phone call, Mary!

There are those who would say that I am being silly about a 15-year-old boy. Over-protective, they would accuse. Over-protective? About wanting to know where my son is in case of an emergency? About wanting to know that he is safe? About wanting from him the courtesy of communication? He said he would be home

31

at midnight and he wasn't. What about his sense of responsibility? So here I sit, unable to sleep, wondering
how I will handle this newest wrinkle in relationship
with my teen-aged son. And he? Sleeping soundly, as if
nothing out of the ordinary has occurred.

Was that how it was with Jesus that time when you
all went up to Jerusalem for your annual Passover celebration? Remember when he was lost, when you and
Joseph searched and searched for him because he
wasn't where he was supposed to be?

You were returning to Nazareth and, though you
had not seen him at the gathering of the caravan, you
assume he is there somewhere and so it is only when
you are a full day's journey out of Jerusalem that you
and Joseph realize that he is not with you. There is
nothing to do but to leave the caravan and retrace your
steps back to Jerusalem.

Along the way you speak little and then only to reassure one another. "Jesus is big for his age," Joseph
says, "and he is pretty level-headed. He probably
started out with the caravan forming next to us, realized
his mistake, turned back and even now is waiting right
where we told him to meet us."

"Yes," you agree, but privately you are thinking,
"If he is so level-headed, how did he get into the wrong
caravan in the first place?"

"There's no need to worry, Mary. We'll find him
soon."

"I know, Joseph." But your stomach doesn't know
and it is churning signals which cause you to scan the
sides of the road compulsively, afraid of what you
might discover and yet more afraid not to know.

By the time you reach Jerusalem it's late and you're
both exhausted. You go to the place you were to meet
with Jesus but he is not there. After talking it over, you

decide to spend the rest of the night at an inn and get a fresh start in the morning. Neither of you sleeps well nor are you able to find comfort in each other's arms. You awaken, dress quickly, purchase some bread and cheese and leave the inn, searching out any relatives or friends with whom Jesus might have lodged. But there is no sign of him. That night is a repeat of the first except that you are both nearly sick with worry. Now you cling to one another in wordless embrace, afraid to chance what conversation might reveal. Besides, all your words, and Joseph's too, are for Yahweh. It is with him that you plead and beg and bargain. "Anything but this, Yahweh. Anything. He is but a boy. Keep him safe . . . let us find him soon . . . Yahweh, don't abandon us now. Please, Yahweh, please . . ." You fall asleep in each other's arms.

The next morning, Joseph is first to rise and dress. You watch him, thinking that it is really his fault. Jesus belonged with the men. So why hadn't he made sure that Jesus was with them? Joseph interrupts your thoughts grumbling that he's going to the baker to buy some food while you dress. He goes out the door thinking that his assumption that Jesus was with Mary in the caravan would never have happened if Mary didn't encourage Jesus to hang around the women so much. Other boys his age knew where they belonged, why not Jesus?

Joseph returns with barley bread and yogurt. You break off a bit of the bread and dip it into the yogurt but you have no appetite though you note that Joseph's appetite seems little affected. "Unless you want everyone to know what you ate for breakfast, clean the yogurt out of your beard. And then, let's go. We're wasting time as it is." Joseph opens his mouth to respond, thinks better of it and simply does what you demand. At last you leave the inn to search any remaining places you can think of, each of you being studiously polite, deferring to the other with maddening courtesy because neither of you really knows where to look next. The sun is at midday when you finally get a clue from a passing acquaintance who tells you he's heard that some youth is in the Temple astounding the teachers with his knowledge. "It's worth a try," he urges. So you go and you find him there in the Temple.

Nevertheless, you march right up to him and demand to know why he has done this thing to you. "Your father and I have been searching everywhere for you!" He regards you calmly for a few seconds and then quietly asks why you were looking for him. "Did you not know I must be about my Father's business?" For a moment you are absolutely speechless but you recover quickly and tell him that you will talk about this later, that now he is to come with you immediately. He obeys. Joseph is fortunate enough to find a merchant caravan on its way toward Nazareth. Finally, the three of you are on your way home.

The constraint between you and Joseph disappears in the relief that your son is safe and sound. During the journey, you are wise enough to talk through some of the feelings you've had these past days and so free yourselves of any guilts or resentments. Your gratitude to Yahweh is heartfelt and you include him in your decision on how to handle the situation. Jesus, though a little subdued, is eager to please you both and responds with good grace to whatever you ask of him. By the time you reach home, you and Joseph have decided on a course of action. We don't know exactly what it was but it must have been effective for we read that Jesus was obedient to you and "advanced in wisdom and age and favor before God and man."

Writing to you this morning so calmed me that I

was able to get a few hours of sleep after all. My son got up this afternoon. Without prompting, he cleaned his room, emptied the trash and swept the patio. After dinner this evening, he did the dishes. Then we talked. He couldn't call because he spent all his money. At his friend's house they all got to talking and he forgot because they were talking about "God and politics and stuff." Well, Mary, I imagined what you might have said to your son and so I told mine that while I appreciated his concern about his "Father's business" that "business" was mine, too. I told him I stood responsible to God not only with him, but for him, until such time as he was ready to live independently of me. In the meantime, I grounded him for a month. May he grow in "wisdom and age and favor before God and man" also.

Holiday Tears

The holidays have come, wrapping themselves round these weeks like brightly colored tinsel. Work-a-day sounds are filtered through tinkling bells and caroling children. Joy is posted everywhere. I go through the daily motions of the season but my heart is not engaged in even the anticipation, let alone the preparation.

My mother died this past year, Mary. I meant to talk to you about it but, at the time, there seemed so much else to do, so many arrangements to be made, so many people to notify or talk with. Then the world came calling and caught me up in its rush and I had no time to sit down and share with you. Probably, I just didn't think of you as a woman connected to a birth mother and all that such a relationship implies. Instead, I was getting used to being an orphan. Oh, not in any self-pitying or dramatic sense. Just that I was no longer the daughter of someone whom I could call for a recipe or drop in on anytime just to chat about nothing. No longer was I the daughter of someone whose ideas of perfection were such that I lived up to them by simply being who I am.

She wasn't perfect, Mary. No more so than Anne, your mother, was. She mumbled about me sometimes to my sisters, as she did about them, to me. And we more than mumbled about her to each other, especially that last year of her illness when we all experienced the frustrations, anxieties, misunderstandings and denials that go along with the process of caring for a dying parent. But she was our mother. She was my mother. And I miss her so, as you must have missed Anne.

That first year, after your mother's death, as Hanukkah, the Festival of Lights, approached, did you feel untouched by it all? Just wishing it would be over so you could get back to your regular routine? Did you have moments when you simply felt at loose ends with nothing more important to do than stare off into whatever space was before you?

Here it is, two days before Hanukkah. You've brought out the special lamps for the celebration but they remain unpolished. You've washed and bleached the table covering, ground the barley into flour, prepared the cinnamon-spiced goat cheese, cleaned the house (though not as thoroughly as you promise yourself you will after the holidays) and now you've finally gotten round to letting down that hem in Jesus' sabbath gown. You break the thread off and wind it back onto the spindle, placing it in the box that Joseph has made for your sewing supplies. Rising from your chair you are startled by the noisy entry of Jesus and Joseph into the house. Your husband is smiling and nodding at your son who, laughing, comes running to you. "Papa says I can polish the lamps. I know how. Grandma used to let me help. Please, Mama. I'm big enough."

You hesitate for a moment, look at Joseph, then back to Jesus' eager face. "I suppose so. But first, fold and put your robe away." He snatches it and begins rolling it up on his way to his sleeping alcove where he stops, turns and asks, ''Are we going to have goose, Mama? Grandma always cooked the best goose for Hanukkah.'' The memory tugs at his tongue and he licks his lips before ducking behind the curtain.

Joseph crosses the room and stands before you. ''He's right, you know, Mary.'' His arms go around you and you lean into his shoulder, wetting it with a spillover of tears. ''It's Anne, isn't it, Mary?'' he whispers into your hair. ''A year ago, she was here, trying to help even though her strength was so low she was more a hindrance than a help. Remember, Mary? We knew she was going then, and you were willing to let her go. I know you miss her but don't try to grab her back now. You'll only hurt yourself. And the boy, too, Mary.''

You press into his shoulder and let his comfort warm you but from the empty spaces inside you a word forms and by the time it reaches your lips it is a mantra and you whisper, ''mother . . . mother . . . mother . . .''

''Come, Mary, let's lie down for a while. Jesus can polish the lamps in the workshop in case any customer comes walking in.'' He leads you into your sleeping room and, as you crumple down onto the bed, he goes to fetch Jesus and get him started on the lamps. When he returns, he lies down beside you and gathers you into his arms, smoothing back your hair, kissing the salty tears from your closed eyes until, finally, lulled by his soft murmurings, you fall asleep.

Later, you slowly glide into wakefulness on the hum of a child's Hanukkah song whose melody has tendrilled from dream into the next room. You lie there a moment, listening to Jesus' voice get louder as he adds a few words here and there and then you hear Joseph's deep voice softly singing along. You rise, straighten your hair and your gown and step through the curtain to join your family.

They are both at the table, Joseph bent over, trimming a new wick, Jesus dreamily polishing the special lamp. And not, you notice, doing too good a job of it. You smile at your men, big and little, and begin to hum along with them. Joseph looks up inquiringly and you go to him. "I'm alright. I guess the little girl in me didn't die with my mother. I still really miss her." Joseph takes your hand and presses it to his cheek as you turn to Jesus and tell him to run to Aunt Tabitha's house and ask her if she'd like to go to market this afternoon."

He throws his polishing rag down, knocks over his chair as he scrambles out of it. "I know she will. She loves the market place. And Mama," his voice gentles, "I'm sorry about what I said. About Grandma and the goose. You make good goose, too." You reach out to give him a quick hug before he spins off and races out the door.

"Walk!" Joseph yells as you bend to right the overturned chair. You touch the haphazardly polished lamp and recall how you and your mother always did this chore together, but the memory, instead of hurting, comforts you. "Joseph, do you remember that time when Mother went to light the sabbath lamp only she closed her eyes at the last moment and ended up trying to light the salt cellar instead?" He nods and you both laugh and then, wonder of wonders, the echo of your mother's laughter joins yours and her presence is all around you.

Perhaps, Mary, it is only when we have truly opened ourselves to the pain of loss that we can create within ourselves the space for the continuing presence of our mothers, and all our loved ones, to live on in and around us. Hanukkah is about miracles, so is Christmas—about the miracle of all of us connected to Yahweh and, through him, to each other.

A Woman Alone

One time when I visited my mother, she talked a good deal about my father who had been dead for ten years then. A little self-consciously, she recounted a dream she'd had the night before involving her and my dad, a dream which was both a hymn to their shared sexuality and a repressed desire for a return to her days and nights of human loving. My mother was 70 years of age, Mary, and she told me that she still mourned the loss of the gift, that part of herself, that expressed physical bonding which pleasured them both.

She began to wander through her memories, selecting one, then another: "In the evening, he always sat here (patting the place beside her on the couch) right next to me...There was never enough money but somehow...Remember when he built that room for Bobby (pointing through the dining room to an enclosed side porch)...and the alphabet blocks he made for you?"

"Of course, he wasn't perfect," she'd say at some point, but her tone belies her words and softens them

41

into a girl-sweet smile savoring again her dream of the night before.

We sat in comfortable silence, she fingering her well-worn memories like oft-used rosary beads, I thinking of friends and neighbors, women widowed and divorced, now alone, like my mother. So very many of us. But, while my mother was wandering through sunlit meadows, I stumbled into a shadow forest, remembering those first difficult years after my own loss. Then I wondered why my memories included nothing of you at that time, especially since you had lost a husband while you were still relatively young. Legend tells us that Joseph died before Jesus was grown, but nothing else. It adds up to a silence so complete that I am just now beginning to realize the measure of it.

There must have been an official mourning period. When it was over, and friends and neighbors had taken themselves and their empty food bowls home, how did you manage to stitch the hours into new patterns?

Routine carries you through the first weeks, those daily underpinnings of living that wait on no one's grief. Washing, mending, cleaning, bartering, meals, all the bits and pieces that make up the ordinary, that stave off the reality of your situation until your emotions can cope with it. There are slips: placing a third plate on the table, then snatching it away; hearing a footstep that isn't there anymore; turning to ask Joseph if he can fix the wobbly table leg again, hearing only your own words drop to the floor, shuffling through the dust for an answer that will never sound.

And there is Jesus, half-grown, a comfort to you most days, almost an intrusion on others. You are deeply concerned about him, and about your ability to raise him alone, to bring him into full maturity. Though he has placed his small feet carefully into Joseph's footprints, fashioning a lopsided stool by himself for the first time, intoning table grace and other blessings which only males in your tradition may do, he did lose one of Joseph's awls, and forgot to milk the goat last night.

You boundary the edges of your mind with psalms, dozens and dozens of them, over and over again, and then one night, you crawl into the bed which you have banked with pillows to reduce its size. You turn and back up against them, a sorry substitute for the warm and yielding flesh of Joseph, but a tiny comfort, nonetheless. You listen to Jesus settle into sleep while you stare, wide-eyed, into the darkness, your mind a sandstorm of griefs and worries that no prayer will calm. There's little food left, no wine at all, only one denarius in the waist-pouch Joseph had always carried. Even in the best of times there had never been more than a few coins to fill it. And now it would be emptied completely.

Tears sting at your eyes. You blink them back but they refuse your denial and you twist yourself over, convulsively grabbing a pillow and burying your sobs into it. "Joseph, Joseph . . . please . . . what am I to do . . . how . . . Joseph . . ." The spasm finally subsides and you turn upon your back, leftover tears trailing into your hair. A part of you is dying. And somehow you know it.

You are poor, encumbered with a growing boy, no matter the circumstances of his birth. No other man will want to marry you. Not when there are so many lithe, young girls with swollen dowries to enhance their desirabilities. No, Joseph was special, a good and unusual man. And he is gone. With him has gone a relationship you will never duplicate.

This night you realize fully what you have lost, what your body has lost. In the morning, you will rise, exhausted, but accepting the future, accepting yourself as a widow, alone, without the comforts and pleasures of a husband. Through Joseph, Yahweh had provided much. You thank him. And as you turn back to snuggle up against the pillows again, you take your memories of Joseph out of the box you had locked them into at his death, and you place them on a shelf within yourself to be as frequently dusted and enjoyed as you need them to be.

So late I come to realize fully that you too knew the grief of losing a husband, of wondering if anyone could ever take his place, of wondering, finally, how you would survive without him. But you do, Mary, you do. And so will we all.

Growing Pains

It is nearly midnight, and I am sitting up savoring the silence of a sleeping house. This time when all the children are abed and windows and doors shuttered and secured against night distractions has always been a special time for me. Special because, as the day winds itself down into silence, I sense the sounds of my heart taking shape so that I can finger them and ponder them and wonder at things hidden there.

Mary, do you remember when Jesus was a little boy? Chattering at the well with some of your neighbors one day, you shook your head in gentle exasperation over the still fresh memory of his being marched home to you by old Isaac whose fig tree Jesus and his friends had robbed of its first ripe fruit. Sarah, sage and kindly, clucked sympathetically (her great-grandson had been the first to climb the tree that morning) and then predicted: "You think you have problems now ...just wait...now you have little problems...later will come big problems." And the other women present

45

nodded their heads and murmured solemn agreement. Remember?

Sure enough, the years roll by and you have cause to recall that conversation more than once. Jesus, in adolescence and young manhood, experiments with being human. It's normal and natural. But you can't help fretting a bit. Nazareth is a large enough town to have some cultural variety. And some of Jesus' friends, newer friends, seem not to observe strict adherence to the mosaic law. You worry. And then there is Rebecca. A nice girl, but Jesus' conversation begins to seem sprinkled with her name. You wonder. And that night when he didn't come home until the wee hours of the morning, you never did discover where he was or what he was doing.

And the neighbors always have instant advice ready. One suggests to you that you share too close an intimacy with your son. "It's not normal," she says. "He needs a man. Why don't you send him over to Jacob's? He's good with the boys." You smile and say nothing. Privately you think that the farther you can keep Jesus from Jacob the better. And the woman who offers to speak with Jesus, to tell him he should help his mother more. "He's too much with the rabbi, Mary. With no husband, you need help. Jesus should take more responsibility." Again you smile, and say nothing.

You talk with your son. Occasionally you yell at him. Your standing in the community has never been very good and there are times when it appears that Jesus is doing nothing to enhance it. You pray a lot. You remind Yahweh that Jesus is his son, too. "You take over, Yahweh, I don't know how the son of God should act. You tell him." But nothing happens except that suddenly Jesus becomes less communicative. He stops sharing his thoughts with you. His friends come around less often. He seems to spend most of his free time alone.

The neighbors take up the slack and you hear whispered phrases here and there: "Jesus was seen talking with a girl in public, and not so nice a girl, either . . . Jesus, you know, Mary's son? He questioned the authority of the rabbi . . . hear he's not so welcome in the synagogue . . . he's a strange one, that Jesus . . . poor Mary, what that woman has to bear."

You keep your own counsel, Mary. You neither believe nor disbelieve the things you hear. Jesus is a man now. His business and his lifestyle belong to him. Though sometimes in the silence of the night you empty your heart of all the things hidden there and sort through them as I have been doing, during the day you go about your tasks and community responsibilities with your head high and a smile for the people around you.

Finally comes the evening when Jesus tells you that he is leaving, going away for awhile, into the desert. He's still not sure of his way, he tells you. His friends have long since gone into apprenticeships and occupations, into marriage, some have even fathered children by this time. He only knows, he says, that this is not for him. So he will be leaving in the morning before dawn. He's not sure when he will be back. "And say goodbye to Rebecca for me," he calls as he goes out to sit for a time before going to bed.

After he is gone, friends come gradually to know of his absence. Some stay to sympathize, others scurry to tell the latest: "Jesus has gone and done . . . left his mother high and dry . . . and her without a husband to care for her . . . she's not getting any younger, you know . . . he just up and left . . . his own mother . . . well, I always said that boy didn't have a chance . . . all that traveling they did in the beginning . . . Mary did

her best, poor thing . . . now, my Joshua wouldn't think
of going off to do his own thing . . . he has a sense of real
responsibility . . .''

You hear, and you don't hear. You take in washing
to make ends meet. You manage. And you wait. You
listen quietly while other mothers brag about their
sons' accomplishments, about their grandchildren and,
when asked, say that Jesus is fine, ''just fine.'' You
spend more and more time talking with Yahweh, assuring him, too, that Jesus is ''just fine.''

And then, there he is: Jesus, come home. You can
hardly speak for the joyous laughter that bubbles up
and out of you as you bustle around, aches and pains
forgotten in the celebration of your son returned. Your
spirit soaks up his words and glows in wonder at the
thoughts and feelings he shares with you over the next
few days. You tell him of an upcoming wedding and
ask him to go. He knew the family and agrees. And at
Cana you nudge your son, the one who's ''just fine,''
into public life.

After a glass of Jesus' new wine, you leave the party
to the young people, and walk slowly home. And you
remember that moment at the well, with Sarah and her
little and big problems and you smile. ''No problems,
Sarah,'' you whisper to your long-departed friend,
''just the process of becoming human, of testing and
learning what it means to become fully a person, the
son of God.''

Will They Ever Leave?

The summer has been long and hot, one of those energy-sapping, temper-cracking sort, made even more so by a house full of adult children. The economy is such that our children are not only remaining home longer but many, finding it financially impossible to live away from home, are returning after having been gone for one, two or even six years. Most of us parents were not prepared for this experience.

My religious tradition has you, Joseph and Jesus sculpted in a spruced up, every sabbath-best fold in place Christmas card. The three of you, when Jesus is old enough, stand closely together in perfect nuclear harmony. Other Christian traditions do the same, although many of them tell of other children that you and Joseph produced after Jesus' birth. ''Four boys and several girls'' they usually say.

This is not a theological treatise, so no matter. But, even so, yours was probably a parallel cousins culture where the raising of children was shared in some manner, so that you conceivably had certain children eating and sleeping over, growing up as freely in your house as in their own, calling you Mom and presuming upon the privileges which they continue to assume right into adulthood.

The wedding feast at Cana is several weeks past and Jesus is still at home. It has not been unpleasant having your son back with you, though you are beginning to tire of the extra laundry, lugging the heavier loads back and forth to the river, and the unexpected guests who drop in to stay for supper, and then stay on to talk with Jesus. The morning you trip over Jesus' sandals in the middle of the room for the umpteenth time you kick them across the floor and mutter ''Great Jehovah, when is he going to leave!'' But he stays.

Then Ephraim and Jacob, back from their fishing trip, move in. (Ephraim's parents are dead and Jacob's house is overflowing so they've come to bunk in.) You accept their gift of fish with gratitude, welcome them and double your own work load because of them. Everything is fine for a few days. The three young men are in good spirits and seem appreciative of you and each other. But soon enough they all settle in and seem to take for granted the meals, laundered robes, made-up beds, swept floors, furniture they re-arrange to suit their own purposes always having been pushed back into place by the time they get up the next morning.

When Phillip and his wife arrive from Galilee and he asks if Martha can remain with you while he goes on a mercantile trip to Egypt, you gladly say yes, thinking that at least you will have a little help. But Martha is with child, her first one, and you soon discover that she fears exerting herself too much. You do notice, though, that she is capable of sitting up late and listening with rapt attention to Jesus' ideas.

You find yourself going outside after the dishes are

done to sit on a rock behind the house. You yearn for bed but the hum of conversation in the small house won't allow you to sleep. Ephraim comes out and looks for you. You brace yourself, hoping he won't see you. But he does and comes over to make conversation. You wait, knowing what is coming. Sure enough, it's Jesus and his locusts again. Ephraim can't stand them and it irritates him beyond belief when Jesus pops a few into his mouth. Ephraim finally leaves and you wearily slip to the ground and lean against the rock.

Yesterday it was Jesus. "They just can't see it," he had exclaimed. "I tell them over and over, give them parables to explain it and still they don't get it. They are worse than little children. I tell you, Mother, Martha understands more than they do!" And then, a couple of hours later, Jacob had come to complain about Ephraim's always managing to get the largest portion at supper. In fact, he was barely speaking to Jacob now. Martha, too, had taken to weaving little innuendoes into her conversation about the young men's habits, even complaining about Jesus' way of rising early to go out and pray before sunrise. "I wouldn't mind if he weren't so noisy about it," she had whined.

"Yahweh, oh Yahweh," you sigh. "You should be here in the flesh. It is not so easy with the big ones. When they were little they would fight and make up and always be friends. Now they don't fight so much, but they are not friends all the time either. They continually burden me with their prejudices and intolerances of one another. They are so different from each other.

"And they break with the old way. Even Jesus. Especially Jesus. Martha, sitting there after supper listening to the men, instead of doing the dishes! Yahweh, what is your world coming to that such things should be happening in my house?"

You raise your head, catch sight of the stars, look

around you and hear yourself repeating softly the words of Psalm 133. The very idea of the psalm soothes your soul and you repeat it: "How good, how delightful it is for all to live together like brothers and sisters: fine as oil on the head, running down...." Suddenly you stop, sit up straight, smile and repeat the opening line of the psalm again.

"Yahweh, your world will happen in my house when we, all of us, become to each other as brothers and sisters! But," you think, "how can that be when I am mother to them, when they are children to me?" You sit absolutely still, the words of the psalm scooting back and forth across your mind. Somehow, somewhere, there is an answer there. "Brothers and sisters . . ." Like a litany you repeat the words over and over. "But why are we not acting like brothers and sisters?" you ask Yahweh and yourself. "They came home, these grown-up children, and all of them are capable adults elsewhere. . . . Yet after three days or a week, they've all settled into the same places they were when they were little. And I? I respond by nourishing them as I did those many years ago. But that's not what they need, is it, Yahweh?"

You stand up, brush the sand off and walk back to the house. You feel your mind expanding, bursting with one insight after another. "It will take time, Yahweh. Your miracles always do, you know. But I think that if I let go of my mothering them, then they can let go being mothered by me. As long as they stay with me, I will tell them that. And I'll tell them they need to do some of the work, too. Eventually we will, with your help, see each other as persons and respond to each other as sisters and brothers, truly your children."

You sigh again as you open the door to enter your house. One way of nourishing gives way to another, which ultimately gives way to freedom for us all.

What a Curious Culture

Last week I attended an anniversary celebration for some former neighbors of mine. There were a number of guests at the party whom I had not seen for several years. At one point, after we had all inquired about each other's children and their present whereabouts and activities, someone turned to me and asked what I was doing these days to amuse myself now that my kids were nearly all grown and gone from home. I answered that I was attending college, preparing myself for new roles and looking forward to the time when I could give myself to new directions. One of the guests, male, winked at me and commented that keeping busy until the grandchildren arrived was a good idea. I protested his remark and there ensued a discussion on the roles of women, the general opinion being that ''once a mother, always a mother'' and that ''being a grandmother was the reward for having been a mother.'' Realizing that nothing I, or the other women present, had said was being accepted seriously, I excused myself to leave the

group when one of the men slipped his arm about my
waist and said: "Just wait . . . when those grandchildren start coming you'll settle down and have a lot
more fun with them than you are with all those books
and things."

What a curious culture we have. On the one hand,
we women are told our place in society, including
church, and on the other, we are admonished to emulate you, to accept God's call, to say: "Yes, Lord." Your
culture was far more restrictive than ours is yet had you
remained in your place would you have become the
mother of God's son? If you had not had the courage to
step out of place could Yahweh's plan for you ever have
been worked out? Would that courage have transmitted
itself to Jesus so that, during his public ministry, he
would have stood against the rigid mores and customs
of your time to call women to himself in friendship and
discipleship, to call them from kitchen and bedroom to
become whole and integrated persons in relationship to
himself and to his father?

After the wedding feast at Cana, it is written that
"Jesus went down to Capernaum, along with his
mother and his brothers and his disciples; and there
they stayed only a few days." After that Jesus goes on
to Jerusalem, but what of you? You've said good-bye to
him, knowing that you've given him all you could. You
may not be sure that he really knows what he is doing,
you may even be a bit fearful for him but you entrust
him to Yahweh. Certainly you do not tag along after
him. The gospel writers appear to take pains not to
place you amongst his disciples. In fact, during the next
three years of Jesus' life you are mentioned only a few
times and then usually indirectly.

There is some evidence that you return with family
members to Nazareth. Then what? Three years later, you
are in an upper room after your son's death and resurrec-

tion and the others present seem to look to you for leadership, not sentimentally as the mother of Jesus, but as a member, a disciple of the emerging church. What was the path that took you from a little house in Nazareth to an upper room in Jerusalem for the first Pentecost?

From the beginning, you filled your heart with the wonder and the mystery of your son. Even as new reports of his miracles and of his preachings come to Nazareth, you ponder them in relation to this memory or that one. Occasionally you are disbelieving. Sometimes you want to go to him and tell him to be careful. Once, you do go. When you send word to him that you, his mother and his brothers wish to see him, he does not come through the crowd to you but sends the message that "My mother and my brothers are those who hear the word of God and do it." Did you understand that day what Jesus was saying? Or did you take it as a rejection and return to Nazareth loving him but not comprehending his words?

There is evidence that the Jewish practice of separating women from men in the synagogue was not necessarily done during your time. Evidence further suggests that women were not only major benefactors of synagogues but sometimes acted as leaders in them. If that were so, though you could hardly have been a benefactor, perhaps you were a member of such a synagogue and accustomed to a certain equality. Perhaps there, after prayer, you meet for instruction or sharing. Surely Jesus and his teachings are discussed. So, though you are not with him, he is becoming present to you in new ways.

All these things you ponder as you hear about a woman at a well and a woman cured of hemorrhage. Somehow things begin to come together and your conversations with God become more relaxed. "This son of yours, Yahweh, the people follow him in such crowds. You give him power to work miracles. Such miracles. And words, Yahweh, have you listened to him? Always something new he is saying. I don't understand him sometimes but I love him so. And his words feel right. Like you would say. Maybe he is not crazy like some of them say. Just keep a close watch on him, Yahweh. Keep him safe from his enemies.''

Gradually you realize that something is happening within you, a new confidence, a new direction. You cease being defensive of Jesus and fearful of some of the things he does and says. Some of these things you and he had even discussed in the past. Suddenly there is more room for Mary within you and you discover that you are being asked more and more to participate in groups, to speak with others, to minister in new ways to new people.

You meet women who have traveled with your son and from them you learn that he is according a new dignity to women. You allow these thoughts to work within you, to become part of your prayer, to spill over into your own words, to flow through you to others. In the process you are growing, moving into new roles that we, the women of today, can truly emulate. We can, with you, say ''Yes, Lord'' in as many different ways and at as many different times in our lives as he wants us to.

A Heart That Sings

A few days ago I met someone whom I hadn't seen for several years. He was once very important to me and to the living of my life, so important that eventually I took pains not to see him, not even to think of him. It was not easy because I loved him very much. But for various reasons there was to be no future together for us. And yet, in the very act of loving, and of being loved, I discovered a future.

Mary, were you ever in love? Really in love? Oh, I know you loved Joseph. But surely there was a great deal of gratitude there for the compassion, the kindness, the security he afforded you and your son. But was he your first love? Or your one, true love? The one for whom your heart sang twenty-four hours a day? Whose glance brought natural blush to your cheeks and energizing currents to your blood? Whose very being gave undreamed of dimensions to the height and depth and breadth of your soul?

Such a love came to me in middle age. I had lost a

husband, was concerned with raising the children of
that marriage and looking for nothing beyond the suc-
cessful completion of each day. It came to me slowly
and unbidden. I became lost in the wonder of it and I
knew only that I had entered the springtime of my life.
But love has its own seasons. Winter came before autumn and summer came not at all.

When Joseph died, you were certainly no more
than middle-aged for your time and culture. Jesus was
hardly a small child then. He was probably not much
younger than you were when you married Joseph.
What happened then, Mary? After the grief had spent
itself, after the void within you had shrunk to a small
but permanent part of you? Did there ever come a day
when, on the way to the village well, in the market
place, at synagogue on the Sabbath, you suddenly felt
your breath catch in that special recognition of a certain
person? No matter that you had never spoken. The on-
set of such love is sudden and is not born in words. It
could have been someone as close to you as Joseph of
Arimathea might have been. Perhaps a casual acquaintance suddenly took on new and different stature in
your heart. Even a stranger, someone not of your culture.

It's not really important, I suppose. What matters is
whether you experienced the fullness of being a woman
so in love that the very hills danced for you and the desert sands greened and the moon rose as your personal
medallion. What matters is that silly, sentimental songs
became profound statements of love, that suddenly
you heard the Song of Solomon read with a depth of
understanding that left you almost gasping.

Projection? Yes. But a projection born of my own
experience and that of scores of other good and godly
women. Surely as valid as that of church fathers who
defined you from their own projections of what a

woman, mother of their god, should be. You came to us a slim, virginal mother as non-aging, non-wrinkling, non-sagging as a piece of modern polyester. They drained you of blood and passion and then offered you to us as a role model.

Mary, I can live with that no longer. Projection, yes, but a sharing, too, of an experience that enlarges the heart to bursting and expands the soul to spaciousness. It is a feeling of well-being, of God-being. For some fortunate persons it leads to a permanent and viable relationship. For others of us, myriad circumstances combine and we find ourselves traveling a road of agony as deep as was our joy. Our hopes, our dreams, our expectations are shattered and we plunge into an abyss of loneliness, even bitterness.

It takes a while but eventually our spirits, limp and wrung-out though they be, do rise. Then the wonder is that we survived that incredible experience of ecstasy and anguish. But survive it we do and gradually we come to recognize that what we thought was a broken heart is now a more gentle heart. The soul we thought shrivelled and withered blossoms into a beauteous place of compassion and understanding. Having been absorbed into the universe by a great and impassioned love, we emerge with the capacity to embrace that universe with graciousness.

Mary, full of grace born of the passion of living fully this human life with which we are all gifted, I embrace you in spirit and walk tall without apology for my woman's heart.

The Gift of Laughter

Today leaped out of the darkness with hardly pause for sunrise and threw thunderous tantrums throughout the morning. By this afternoon, the humidity, like un-shed tears, has swollen the already high temperatures to record-breaking levels. This evening, the heat lingers and there is no respite in sight.

I had expected two guests for lunch today. They never came. So I sat down at my specially prepared table and ate alone. Thinking about it, I am sure it amounts only to a confusion in communication. Still. . .

This afternoon I had planned a birthday celebration dinner for my sister. The party involved twelve people and was to begin at 4:30. Five guests arrived on time. The others straggled in between 6:00 and 7:00 with various excuses, most of them valid, I suppose. The teen-aged boys had consumed far more than their share of the meat by then so I had to send my daughter for more. The potatoes were overbaked, the vegetables soggy, the salad wilted. The candles on my sister's cake would not stay lit until we removed one child who had been unobtrusively blowing them out.

Everyone left soon after they had shared the cake and, I confess, I was not unhappy to see them go. I then busied myself with clean-up while muttering my way into a self-pitying depression, a warm, soggy one in which I could self-righteously wallow for a few hours. The phone rang and, thinking it might be serious, I answered. A friend was calling to inquire if I would like some company. I didn't, but she insisted and would be here within ten minutes with another friend in tow.

It is now close to midnight. My friends have long since departed and I feel human again. By the time they and I had shared a glass of wine and I had recounted my day which, in turn, prompted each of them to share similar experiences, we were so convulsed with laughter that my perspective changed entirely. I have been thinking about shared laughter this past hour, and about sanity.

You must have laughed a great deal, Mary. How else could you have lived the life you did? How else transcend the poverty, the humiliations, the rejection, the pain and the sorrow? How else hold on to faith, to hope, and, yes, even love? Yet, if taken literally, the gospels and tradition indicate that your last moment of joy occurred when you and Joseph, realizing that Jesus had been lost for three days, discovered him at the temple in Jerusalem. After that, it's all downhill! Nor can I recall any art that shows you laughing. Some has you smiling but always with the child Jesus.

I imagine you in the company of friends, perhaps Martha and one or another of the Marys, all of you laughing in order to right a world gone insane. You, particularly, laughing to exercise the frustration and the grief and the pain of a life whose promise seems never to have materialized. You are middle-aged, widowed, probably dependent upon others for food and shelter. You are sometimes unfamiliar with the man the child of your womb has become, fearful for his reputation, for his very life. Somehow you must walk these days, lose their concerns and worries in sleep at night.

You discover strength in the community of women who support your son, who have listened to him, heard him, accepted his teachings and grown in dignity. In these women, whom Jesus has made aware of their personhood, you discover your own personhood. When Martha shares with you that she has confessed Jesus to be "Christ, the Son of God, who has come into the world," you know somehow that the promise of your life is yet to be.

You are comfortable with the complete faith and dedication of these women of Jesus, and at ease with the independence, the assertiveness, the sense of equality they share with the men around your son. In the company of Martha and her sister, Mary, of Lydia, of Joanna, of Mary Magdalene, you enter into a deepened sense of yourself.

Perhaps, of an evening, you might all gather, sip a little wine, and share something of yourselves with each other. You are all women of faith and therefore women of laughter. Even when the talk turns to Jesus, as inevitably it does, and you sift through the dire rumors that are beginning to circulate as your son prepares to go to Jerusalem for Passover, you do not panic. The courage and the humor, the hope and the love of these women sustain you and warm you and still the grief which already begins to whisper deep within you. That night, even as you pray together, there is laughter. And you carry it with you as you go to your bed thanking Yahweh for revealing himself yet again in community.

Tonight, I thank God for community in which we share laughter that heals, imparts courage, underscores faith and restores the ordering of our lives.

When Loved Ones Grow Old

It's Monday morning and clouds, like carelessly piled heaps of soiled comforters, spill down the hills across the valley. There is a smell of rain in the air and brisk breezes shake out dusty trees, readying them for laundering, while birds, the color of weathered clothespins, perch on telephone wires chattering storm warnings to one another.

Monday morning, wash day, the day my mother always did the week's laundry, batches of it, making trip after trip to the backyard to hang every last sock of it up to dry.

Even when my mother was in her 70s, a fragile autumn leaf of a woman, who had to cheat to make up one good washing machine load, she still hung out her few items on the old clothesline. It was a slow-motion exercise for her and we worried that she would stumble, lose her balance, somehow hurt herself, with no one there to rescue her. She steadfastly refused to leave her home, to have a dryer, to be dependent. Some days her

65

attempt at independence delighted us and we affectionately played the game with her, because we loved her.
But more and more often we, who had finally nurtured
our own children into adulthood, encountered in our
own mother another child, a recalcitrant and sometimes stubborn child trying to escape the confines of aging. It hurt. We understood, Mary, but it still hurt.

Frequently, when I was with her and listening with
one ear to the oft-repeated details of her very shrunken
world, I wondered if you were as intimately involved
with elderly beloved ones as so many of us are today.

What about your mother? Anne was not young
when she birthed you, Mary. So the story goes anyway.
Actually we know nothing about your parents, or Joseph's. But if I imagine that Anne had a younger sister,
widowed now, her two children part of the diaspora
movement as so many of your people were at the time,
then I place her in her home in Nazareth with you as her
nearest close relative. Your cousins send money, occasionally come to visit. But you live nearby, you go to sit
with her, you offer the distraction of company.

Most of her friends are gone or too infirm to come
see her these days. So it falls to you to recount the village gossip, to tell her the news that comes in with the
caravans. Sometimes old Auntie Tabitha is present,
alert, conversational. She's swept and tidied her little
house before you arrive and, though her bustling is reduced to a soft shuffle these days, she resolutely prepares lunch, eats with appetite and insists you not help
with the clean-up. ''I'll do them later instead of taking a
nap; maybe I'll fall asleep sooner tonight. Here, let me
wrap up this bit of fish for you. Jesus always liked my
fish. Where is that boy? He hasn't been to see me in a
long while. Why, he used to drop by just to talk. Not
like that John, Elizabeth's son. Always thought he was
a bit weird. . . remember. . .?'' As she begins again to re-

weave the past in the pattern of her own impressions, you quietly clear the table, rinse the dishes, put them away and then, bending to her, gently interrupt her: "Auntie, how about a little rest?" "No, no, not now. Maybe later. You run on, Mary and tell that little Jesus I'm going to bake him that special cake he likes so much. Maybe next week when I feel a little more peppy." Slowly she walks you to the door, holds her face up for you to kiss her and waves you on home. You call back to her, "You be sure and eat something this evening, maybe that leftover fish, and I'll come by for your washing tomorrow."

The next morning, basket in arm, you arrive at Tabitha's house only to find it shut up tightly. You knock on the door once, twice, a third time and call her name. Finally you hear a fumbling at the door and when it is opened you know immediately that the chatty Auntie Tab is gone again. In her place is this faltering question mark of a woman who inches back to her chair and carefully sits down. You put your basket on the floor, cross to her, give her a hug and ask her how she is feeling. "Not so good," she replies in a wisp of a voice. You sit down, forcing yourself to be patient, wondering if there will be a decent spot left at the river this morning, wondering why it always seems to happen when you are busiest. You realize she is speaking and lean forward to catch the rustle of her words: "tired. . . I just wish you didn't have to stop for my washing. . . you do so much for me. . . don't know what I would do without you. . . since your uncle died. . . no one else. . ."

"Oh Yahweh," you sigh. Immediately, her eyes flash up and distinctly she demands: "What did you say, Mary?"

"Nothing," you reply. "Did you eat this morning, Auntie?" "I just don't feel like eating," she says faintly, eyes downcast. A swift jolt of exasperation brings you to

your feet and you mask it by moving briskly to the
kitchen area where you set water on to boil even as you
note the freshly emptied porridge bowl on the edge of
the table. Then you gather in linens and her few clothes
and toss them in the basket with your own. Though
Aunt Tabitha appears lost in a cheerless world of self-
absorption, her defense against a world she is physically
unable to cope with anymore, you know that she is
aware of every move you make. Wash day is hard for
her, a symbol of aging. While all the other women gather
at the river for what used to be a grand convivial time for
her, she must remain at home. Alone. The river is too far
for her painfully swollen ankles, the weather too hot for
her brown parchment-like skin.

You stir the porridge into a bowl and a feeling of
compassion washes away your impatience. Swiftly you
rearrange your day and resolutely tell her to be dressed
and ready an hour before sundown. "Old Rachel
bought spices the other day. Maybe we can barter for a
little. And I hear that old Zechariah will be staying
there. He just came in from Syria." Tabitha nods
slowly, sits a little straighter. "Zechariah, heh? Well, if I
am feeling better. . ." and she drops her head again. But
not before you have caught a glimpse of the spirit of the
17-year-old girl, alive and well, in her eyes. She is there
still, imprisoned by the years, bound by physical limita-
tions, by aches and pains, but ready to fly again at a moment's notice.

Smiling, you pick up your basket, kiss the top of her
head, remind her to be ready and go out the door. "Yahweh, Yahweh, bless old Zechariah and bless these feelings, these so human feelings which call us to life even
when we are old." You chuckle and suddenly the bur-
dens of the day seem lighter. Aunt Tabitha will be ready
on time. Just as we all, somehow, will be ready in our
time, graced by the feelings of youth even into old age.

On the Road to Bethany

The grammar school which all of my children attended celebrated its 25th anniversary a few weeks ago and many of us actively connected with the school's past were guests of honor. A number of us with children now grown to and beyond the quarter century mark had not met in years yet soon after sitting down to the inevitable hot dogs, potato salad and baked beans, we fell back into the old camaraderie of whatever-the-school-needed sense of community that had engaged and sustained us through those years of our children's early education.

They were hectic years but joyful ones. We were so full of faith and hope in ourselves and in our children.

Anyway, Mary, as we chomped our hot dogs and pushed our beans around, we all swapped tales of our kids' successes. Had we not all been old hands at this parenting of adult children, we might have left it at that. But we heard which names were either not being mentioned or were being passed over a little too quickly. Be-

cause most of us had used them ourselves, we recognized the euphemistic phrases that served to gloss over
the flouting of traditional values, that served to camou-
flage selfishness, insensitivity and materialism as independence, sensitivity and practicality.

With gradually deepening honesty we heard from
the mother who, after an argument with her 24-year-
old son, hung a *bon voyage* sign on his bedroom wall and
covered his floor (where she could find space) with a
dozen empty, open grocery bags as a gentle hint. We
heard from the mother whose one daughter had married a twice-divorced man and because he had four children from his previous marriages, had decided to have
none of her own, and whose other daughter and her
husband just bought a beautiful home and felt that they
didn't need children. But I thought of you, Mary, when
one mother told of her son whom she had not heard
from in over three months despite a phone message left
for him to call her. ''And he only lives 20 miles away!'' I
thought of you because a careful reading of the gospels
tells us that Jesus didn't call home either.

The temptation is to believe that there was always
perfect communication between you and your son, that
your faith and hope in him never weakened, that somehow you knew everything was going ahead on some
sort of heavenly schedule. We believe that he visited
with you, embraced you, shared with you his unfolding
mission; that he was attentive to your feelings, avail-
able to you the few times you felt you needed him. But I
guess that is merely a projection of our own desires as
parents. We still wish to place you above the human
condition rather than immersed in it, as we are.

If one thing was clear that day of the anniversary
party, it was that faith and hope in our children may
dim at times but our love for them continues. Like you,
Mary, we all bear heart wounds. But perhaps these

wounds are the swords that prune back and finally cut away the expectations we have of and for our children.

No, Jesus did not call home. And when you went up to Jerusalem to see him, he didn't even come out to greet you, his mother. How badly you must have felt! Because, no matter your rationalizations, no matter how hard you tried to understand and defend him, feelings have a way of seeping out through the most reasoned of arguments. And your feelings are hurting ones. The kind that creep into your throat at night and emerge as a sob, the kind that buzz in your ears with questions of "why?" giving way to "if only I had said or done..." and finally to "what if I went back and what if I demanded..." Your agony replaces itself with anger but after a while that too is exhausted. There is nothing left but the tears, and the decision.

"So, Yahweh, this son of yours, he doesn't want me around. He treats me like a stranger yet. He's so busy running around the countryside. . . and the people, Yahweh, you can hardly get a glimpse of him for the mobs that follow him. For them, he has time! For me, none. What's a mother to do, Yahweh? All these years I have responded faithfully to you. I have done what you asked of me, not always an easy task, as you well know. And now, Joseph is gone, Jesus is gone, all the others, nieces, nephews, friends gone on, too. And you send me no more angels with messages.

"Neither wife nor mother these days. But I see other women, Yahweh, also neither wives nor mothers and they do other things. There's Martha and her sister, Mary. I have met them, and I like them. And I talked with that uppity woman who argued with Jesus. Yes, I heard about that. She got his attention even if I couldn't. If you have no objection, Yahweh, then I think I will go see some of these women who know my Jesus. They are different from the women here. In the meantime, you watch out for our rebellious son. Yahweh, I worry but I will not sit here and cry about it. Amen.''

You feel energized and start bustling around, straightening the house, while making plans to go to Bethany. Without realizing it, Mary, you have rid yourself of expecting anything more of the mother-son relationship. You have taken the first step out of the role of ''Mary, mother of Jesus,'' a role which has defined you for over thirty years, a role which bound you to certain traditions and conventions. Suddenly, you feel neither rejected nor cast off but free—free to pursue new directions and new relationships.

New? A trickle of self-doubt enters your mind and for a moment you stop what you are doing and sit down and experience little fears nibbling away at your surge of confidence. Then you remember Gabriel and the trip to Elizabeth's house and difficulties surrounding the birth of your first-born in a stable in Bethlehem. In your mind's eye you travel down the years making a tally of all the times you felt fear of the unknown before you. ''But I never gave in to it (well, maybe a little here and there) and I never gave up. Always I had faith—faith in Yahweh and in myself. And I am not going to give up now! Jesus doesn't need me in the mothering role anymore. He is his own man now. I will be my own woman now!'' With that you bounce up and continue preparations for your journey to Bethany.

That afternoon, after saying good-bye to people whose lives had once mingled daily with mine, I realized that many of us were on that road to Bethany with you, Mary, slipping out of our parenting roles along the way as best we could. Feeling our expectations of our children, and of ourselves, too, draining away, leaving us a sense of freedom and excitement in traveling the road before us. We begin discovering who we are apart from the world of children, our own and others. We are alive!

Companions on the Way

Recently a friend hosted a luncheon for eight women, including myself. We have all known each other for years, some a little more intimately than others, but each of us had, at one time or another, been deeply present to a profound moment in the others' lives. We had all come a long way this past decade, and we knew it. The conversation was honest, intelligent, witty, and revealed the wisdom, integrity and determination of women whose frustrations and indignations were kept in perspective with laughter—Bethany laughter, Martha laughter, the kind of laughter that only those who have baked the bread and never gotten more than the leftover crumbs of it, can belly up to.

The roads we've traveled have been up and down hills, Mary, much as the road you must have walked to Bethany. The further you go, the more you wonder if this trip is a foolish one. You remember another trip you undertook alone: the one to Elizabeth's when you were pregnant with Jesus. Then, you were flushed with the

certainty of God's plan for you. Then, you knew yourself to be part of Yahweh's design and had only to allow
his plan for you to unfold. You were intimately a part-
ner in his creation, a nurturer of child and husband. The
security of identity was yours and as you walked to Elizabeth's house nothing could touch you. Wrapped in
youth and joy, you were caught up in the mysteries of
your own heart and soul and body. You were full,
Mary, with a radiating innocence that the rigors of life
had not yet dimmed.

But you are no longer young. You feel empty,
lonely and alone. Joseph is dead. Jesus is roaming the
countryside more concerned with strangers than with
you. No angel messenger appears this time to reassure
you. There are even moments when you feel aban-
doned by Yahweh. But the deepening green of the hills
near Bethany draws you, birdsong lifts your spirits, the
smile of a shy, dusty child enchants you and the people,
always the people, encourage you by their very presence on this road. Most of them, you know, are going to
or returning from Jerusalem, which is just a few miles
the other side of Bethany. An energy in them communi-
cates itself to you. You cannot help but respond to the
sense of vitality around you.

When the sun is high and you are only a hill's dis-
tance from Bethany, you stop near a fig tree and carefully ease yourself down upon a grassy spot near a clus-
ter of Canaanite people. There was a time when you
might have felt a little uncomfortable sitting so near
them since, like most of your people, you never placed
yourself in a position where you might socialize with
them. But the road has had its own peculiar camaraderie and you have grown accustomed to sharing your
space and your time with all manner of people. So
when one of the younger women smiles tentatively at
you, you smile back. When she offers you some water,

you gratefully accept it and begin to chat as people do in such situations.

She shyly tells you that she is from the region of Tyre and Sidon and she is returning there from Jerusalem, where she had seen Jesus. "Do you know about him?" she asks. When you answer yes she moves a little closer and begins to tell you about a woman she knows from home, another Canaanite. It seems, the young woman confides, that this woman had left her home with the express purpose of finding this Jesus and asking him to cure her daughter of some mental illness. Finally locating Jesus, she had boldly walked right up to him (in public, no less!) and asked that he cure her child. Jesus ignored her and the men around him advised him to send her off. But the Canaanite woman persisted and so Jesus told her bluntly that he had come only for the Jews. Even though the woman knew she was outside the House of Israel, she pleaded anyway: "Lord, help me." But Jesus rebuked her: "It is not fair to take the children's bread and throw it to the dogs."

"Are you certain he said that to her?" you ask. True, the Canaanites are second-class citizens but you had tried to instill in Jesus that, though he must not run around with them, they were deserving of the common courtesies. The young woman asserts the truth of what she stated and then excitedly runs on: "But wait, the best part is coming because, remember, I told you I know this woman? Well, she's smart and, let me tell you, she always wins an argument. So she never even hesitates. She just looks at this Jesus and says: 'Yes, Lord, yet even the dogs eat crumbs that fall from their master's table.' And then he told her that for saying that, for such a good argument, her daughter was healed! Wasn't that a marvel?"

Startled, you slowly release the breath you had drawn in at the audacity of that unknown Canaanite woman. But the one next to you does not notice. She sits back on her heels, all shyness gone, her face aglow with the excitement of telling you, a Jewish woman, her incredible story. And you sense something different about her. It's not the shyness gone, though that's part of it. No, it's in the tilt of her head, the directness of her eyes, the very posture of her body. Excitement, yes, but something more. You recognize a dignity, a sense of worth you have never before seen in a Canaanite woman. As the young woman rises to return to her people, you rise also, embrace her wordlessly and return to the road.

Only one more hill to go but it wouldn't matter now if there were a dozen. Somehow you have absorbed a sense of something beyond knowing one's place. You walk faster, thinking that maybe there is a plan here, too. ''In my youth, Yahweh, you sent Gabriel to say what your plan for me was and it was in the nature of that plan to unfold with each step following from the previous one. I had only to live it. But now, maybe you think I am matured enough to make my own plan. Well, Yahweh, our son learns that you did not send him only to Jews and I learn that we, women as well as men, Canaanites as well as Jews, must step out of place if we are to become whole persons. Amen.''

We will have our slice of bread, too, Mary.

Outcasts by Ignorance

We buried Michael today. He was young, only 28. I did not know him well. But his parents are part of our church community and so I had seen him, heard about him and understood that he was sick as we prayed for his recovery. His name was put into our bulletin sick list as a reminder to contiune remembering him in prayer. But then that list contains the names of people who have long since been out jogging and lifting weights, let alone appearing at Mass every single Sunday. Somehow, though we talk about it, no one ever really weeds the list unless a specific request is made by the now well person. Like the nine lepers who ran off without thanking your son, they simply slip back into community life.

Last week the phone call came, telling of Michael's death and the times of the services to be held at church. It had been little less than a year since we had been asked to pray for Michael's recovery. Time had slipped away, and so had he. I was told that he had succumbed to pneumonia. Later, in the paper, I read that it was

''pneumonia complicated by a staphylocoeus infec-
tion.'' That euphemism has been around long enough
so that I knew that Michael had died of AIDS. We all
knew. Too late to have been of any real support to him
and his family.

AIDS patients are today's lepers, Mary. They are
shunned and avoided for fear of contagion as if to touch
one were a certain kiss of death. Nothing could be further from the truth. But the belief persists and, in their
most intense agony of pain and suffering, many are left
to go it alone like your son did that terrible night in the
garden of Gethsemane.

In your time, Mary, leprosy was used as a generic
term to cover any form of overt skin disease including
psoriasis, impetigo, ringworm, even, I suspect, a se-
vere case of athlete's foot. Your people did not understand the dynamics of specific contagions and so
treated all skin disease as highly infectious. If the le-
sions did not disappear within a specific period of time,
the victim was shunned, made to live apart from the
community.

One evening, Phillip stops by on his way to re-join
Jesus and the others who are traveling through Galilee
and Samaria on their way to Jerusalem. While you slice
a tomato, heat the olives and put rounds of barley bread
on to bake Phillip tells you about the 10 lepers that Jesus
cured. He adds that only one, a Samaritan, had both-
ered to thank him.

You picture the scene and it warms your heart,
though you are saddened, and uneasy, that your own
people seem not to accept your son with the faith that
foreigners do. Then you think of Absalom. Poor Absalom. You wonder if he's heard about Jesus. You say as
much to Phillip and over supper you tell him about Absalom.

''He was the son of Obadiah and Leah. He was

such a handsome little boy, big dark eyes, black curly hair—and so sunny. He made us all laugh. And he loved Jesus. Everyone used to say, 'You want to find Absalom, look for Jesus.' And Jesus, he really liked that boy . . . spent a lot of time with him . . . playing . . . talking . . . teaching him how to work with the wood. When Absalom married Esther, Jesus made them a nice table and chairs. Ah, that was a wedding! A year later, Esther gave birth. A fine boy named David. But by then the troubles had already started . . .'' Your voice trails off and for a moment you slip back in time.

Phillip gently recalls you to himself and asks what happened. "At first," you continue, "it didn't seem like much. Just little things. That Esther was always a chatterbox but she began to get quieter and quieter. We thought it was her pregnancy. But Absalom, too, began to change . . . became more serious . . . didn't smile so much . . . hardly laughed at all. One day I realized that he wasn't stopping by anymore. Jesus was gone by then but Absalom used to come by just to chat or to see if I needed anything. So I went over to Leah's house to ask after him. At first, she was sort of distant. Leah, my friend! Then she started to cry. Finally she told me that Absalom had the disease. It was on his head and his left arm. She said it was sores and that they were scaly.

"You know the law, Phillip. He had to go show himself to the priests but Esther was scared out of her wits that if he went, they would declare him unclean. Leah said that Esther cried a lot but Absalom was tired of pretending and hiding. And now the sores were spreading. How I wished Jesus was here that day! Maybe Absalom would still be here. He was a fine boy and a good man."

"Did he go, then?" asked Phillip. "Yes," you answer. "He went to the priests and after seven days he was no better and they said that the sores had penetrated his skin, too, so they demanded that he leave. And he did.''

The two of you sit companionably talking of other things until Phillip leaves. You clear the table, do the dishes and then ready yourself for bed. After your prayers, just as you are teetering on the edge of sleep, Absalom's face reassembles itself on the surface of your mind. You see him now as you did that last time, a young man of 19 or 20, head uncovered, beard muffled, torn robe with a small bell tinkling at his waist cincture. He is walking slowly, eyes cast down, every footstep a sounding one. He is headed south, probably toward Samaria. No one walks with him, no member of his family. Not his wife. Nor you, either. He has become untouchable. He has left you all. ''Or is it, Yahweh, that we left him? And if we left Absalom, Yahweh, did we not leave you? Forgive us all.''

Forgive us, too, Mary, for not absorbing and trusting the unfolding knowledge of medicine which Yahweh has blessed us with. So much that your people feared because they did not know better, now is understood and controllable if not always fully curable. Contemporary research proves that we need not ''bell'' our AIDS patients, that we can eat with them and hug them and bless each other with Yahweh's saving grace.

Letting Children Grow

We, the living, experience any number of "deaths" during our pilgrimage through the human condition. Not the least of these are the ones connected with our children's easing or stumbling into adulthood. The process is a painful one for them and for us, who often take on their pain in addition to our own.

We hold out the natal cord and wait for them to cut it. Some do it swiftly, cleanly; others seem to gnaw at it interminably. We are hurt and angry either way: that they did it so decisively or that they did it so clumsily. We tend to deny that they are ready to become autonomous persons; we may even try to jerk the cord back. We bargain with them, and with God about them. But even if we responsibly cajole them, tease them, urge them, perhaps threaten them with dire consequences if they don't finally snip that cord, we are depressed when they take us at our word.

I have been thinking about this process lately because I am living through it again. Watching one of my daughters catching hold of womanhood and trying to fit it to herself, I realize it has not been easy for her or for me. It isn't that I would deny her her own destiny, her own autonomy. Not at all. It is more that sometimes I feel so afraid for her, want to spare her the consequences of certain decisions she seems to be making (or not making), want to spare her the pain that seems inevitably hers if she continues as she is.

And you, Mary? How did you manage to live through it all? You must have suffered terribly for your son. The process was a long one, wasn't it? Remember when you went up to Jerusalem and Jesus refused to see you, even to acknowledge you? You were angry then. He was making such a spectacle of himself, embarrassing you and the rest of the family. You only wanted to talk some sense into him, take him home, reason with him, maybe suggest some alternatives. But he would have none of it, so you returned to Nazareth without him.

Then what did you do? What could you do except continue to love him? You may have denied that what he was doing was really so unusual. People exaggerated. People were jealous. Jesus meant no harm, no matter what some members of the Sanhedrin said. He was a good boy—different, more sensitive than most, but a good boy, nonetheless. He would settle eventually, marry, give you grandchildren. But he didn't. Your heart knew the truth long before your mind would admit to it.

You try not to think about him. But there he is, a heaviness in everything that you do. You begin to slow down a bit, until it is taking three days to do what you used to accomplish in two. An unfocused depression has settled upon you like a well-fitting cloak, and you can't shake it off. You dream his face at night; occasionally you wake, get up, pace the floor until dawn. You find yourself talking to him with only the walls for audience. Your eloquence is unbounded. You convince yourself, so you think you can convince Jesus to give up this insane life he has chosen. If only he would listen.

At Bethany, things go better for you. Martha, her sister, Mary of Magdala, the mother of James and John, these women open their arms and their hearts to you. You draw strength from them, but it is not enough to shield you from the rumors, thick as flies, that buzz the countryside. When you hear that Jesus is going to Jerusalem for Passover, you are filled with dread, with a fear so hurting that the constriction in your chest seems to be permanently part of you. You cannot remember when it wasn't there, you cannot imagine it ever not being there.

"Yahweh," you pray, "please, please don't let him do this. Please help him. Save him. You can do it . . . if only you will. Your son! He's your son. He has spoken your word. Yahweh, he has lived for you! Do something . . . please. Never will I ask anything of you again. Just this once. Please save our son. They are going to kill him. I know it. You know it. Please, Yahweh, please . . ." And your tears run mad and plead more forcibly than your words. But Yahweh does not answer.

If it weren't for the women, you think you would die. Curiously, they have more hope than you. But then, he is their rabbi, their lord, for some even, their messiah. He is your son, flesh of your flesh, blood of your blood, and you are drowning in pain.

Word comes finally. They have taken him. Your heart plummets, rearranging everything within you, and suddenly you are outside time and event. Distantly you hear the cries and the wails of the other women. You hear the words of the men, his disciples, giving details, but the sounds are meaningless. Yahweh has, at last, spoken and his word is the gift of numbing calmness to you. Your heart slowly rises to meet your mind and in that instant, you know there will be no reprieve, no turning back. Without question, you accept the fact of your son's decision to live his own life fully and autonomously, even unto death.

As must all of us parents, if we are ever to know new life in our sons and daughters, and in ourselves.

Tomorrow Is Always

My children are at an age when the slivers of their fractured and broken relationships slice into all of us with varying intensities. Not too long ago, I held a daughter in my arms, while she sobbed out convulsions of grief that marked the beginning of the end of all her long held romantic and marital dreams and aspirations. For her, life was over. Nothing would ever be the same again. And she was right. Life, as she had known it, was over; nothing would ever be the same again. She now carried within her the sediment, the ashes, of that grieving. As we both know so well, it is only the beginning.

For weeks afterward, as she worked through the process of collecting the bits and pieces of herself together, I found myself experiencing the rekindled fires of my own grievings. I remembered when I felt that if only I could touch the hem of your son's robes I would be healed, but I couldn't find him anywhere for a while. Now I realize that you had not even that promise.

Jesus' trial, though hurried, probably took longer than the gospel accounts tell us. Though you go when you can to stand witness to him, you take refuge in the ordinary acts, making of them a continuing prayer, feeling somehow that their very normalcy will seal the cracking egg of your world. Passionate indignation at the injustice of it all, at the mindless stupidity of the crowds and the monumental blindness of the magistrates fuels your energy so that you have little time to brood. The verdict will be one of innocence, even of vindication of your son whose gentleness of spirit has never shown so clearly as now. That he should be condemned to die is unthinkable, even unimaginable.

But the unthinkable, the unspeakable happens. Tried as a common criminal, he is assigned a common criminal's execution. Suddenly, where your heart was, there is a huge block of pure pain, immovable, impenetrable pain. In the crowd, surrounded by friends, you scream "No, No . . . please no . . . NO!" To the whole universe you scream it. But no one hears; nothing responds. As your friends lead you back to the house, that scream reverberates within you, bouncing off the huge lump of pain, echoing around it.

That night you sit up. Sleep is impossible. Dry-eyed, you wait for the dawn, trapped in a vise of nothingness. It is a surprisingly calm experience where the passage of time seems outside you; where, if you simply do not move, that hard lump of pain within you will not suffocate you.

Legend tells us that the next morning you were in the crowd that lined the way to Calvary, that Jesus recognized you there, that you wept. I believe that you caressed each other's souls at that moment, Mary, each of you drawing strength from the love that had always flowed in and around and under every nuance of your relationship.

You were able to trudge up the hill and witness what they did to your son. You cling tightly to the women, his friends, who have come from Galilee. Their bodies press around yours and support you. Tears rise from deep within you, slide up and around the unyielding pain in your chest to slip silently, a steady stream sliding down your cheeks, salting your lips before they fall to wet the hands of the women who are holding yours.

Three hours later it is over. This man-child of your womb, indeliby marked on your soul before his very life began, this child whom you birthed in joy and pain, nursed to strength, guided to young manhood, this agonized body of a man whose baby arms you can still feel about your neck, is cruelly dead.

Back at the house, a crowd has gathered. His closest friends are there, and many others, followers of his teachings. Hushed conversation is punctuated by an occasional sob or pain-pitched cry. They come to you, some with words, some with embraces, all with sorrow-colored eyes. From somewhere in the depths beneath your pain you note the anguish, the sense of abandonment in them and soon you are responding, offering them consolation, hugging them back to hope. Then a child grabs at your gown with food-filled hands to keep from falling and you are a little surprised to discover yourself smiling.

Hours later, when only family and close friends remain, one of Jesus' disciples rushes in to tell you that Joseph of Arimathea, that good friend, has obtained permission to take your son from the cross and bury him in a nearby empty grave. "Thank Yahweh!" you exclaim and look for your cloak to follow the man back to Calvary. But it is very close to Sabbath and some of the women from Galilee persuade you to let them go in your stead. Martha hands them clean linen cloths and as the women hurry out the door, she comes to you, puts her arm about your waist and leads you to a sleeping room.

"Now, it is finished, Martha," you murmur. "Yes," she replies, "thanks to Joseph, it is finished. Rest, Mary. When Sabbath is done, we'll go to the tomb. Shalom." She leaves quietly and you lie down, sinking into your body's exhaustion. But sleep does not come. Against your eyelids you feel the stinging seepage of returning tears that does nothing to blur the sudden image of your crucified son. The ball of pain flares within you, sears your throat, devours your voice. Your entire body becomes a seismic inferno of inexpressible grief, the boundaries of your flesh and bone seeming to melt so that you are fused with all the unarticulated pain of the earth itself. It is too much, too much. Helplessly, you feel yourself subsumed into it until somehow, somewhere, time begins again and you cough up great spasms of sobbing. Arms lift you and hold you close as the waves of weeping sweep you, at last, into deep sleep.

The next day you gradually awaken to your heart back in place; the huge pain is gone, dissolved into the fiber of your being. Tentatively you stretch, sit up and warm to the peace flowing through you. The mingled voices of the others in the house bring you to your feet. As you prepare to go out to them an intuition of purpose fills you and through the peace now mixing with the still simmering grief, a bubbling of joy briefly wells up, takes hold of you and, before it recedes, leaves a soft crooning in your heart, "Tomorrow, Yahweh, tomorrow . . ."

My daughter had no such song for, to the young, there seems no tomorrow. But for us, Mary, who have weathered life's aging, tomorrow is always.

The Eternal Moment

Like a length of ribbon you have been braided through my thoughts these past weeks, surfacing at every turn and twist of my mind. The resurrection of Jesus: What was it like for you? There is no account of your meeting with your risen son. Did he come to you? Did you hear of him being seen and go out searching? What happened? How did you feel?

This afternoon I took a long walk through a field alive with tall grasses and clumps of wild flowers. Birds, staircasing tree limbs, were tuning up for their evening vespers as a softly caressing sun prepared to end the "third day," what we call Easter Sunday. Then I remembered that in the religious language of your people "third day" did not have the same numerical meaning that our usage of it has. Rather, it meant "day of victory over the power of evil," the greatest evil being death. Suddenly a thought occurred to me so forcibly that I verbalized it aloud and startled a large lizard into dashing across my path to some primeval place of safety newly touched by spring.

"But, of course!" I shouted to my immediate corner of the universe while birds scattered into brief flight before rearranging themselves in the trees. "The sun," I instructed them, "cannot shut down this day. Not this third day! Not ever! Because this is the day without end on which God overcame evil. It has nothing to do with numbers or numerical exercises defining the how, when, what time that Jesus rose from the dead." I stood there for a moment letting what I had known, but never really absorbed so deeply before, settle into my being, then I turned and began retracing my steps, careful to disturb neither lizard nor bird.

We humans are funny, Mary. We love a mystery—for all of ten minutes! Then we begin trying to unravel it by fitting it into our framework, into our concepts of space and time. But our explanations of the mystery often end up making it seem less credible than if we had never touched it. For instance, we have your son rising on the numerical third day even though the time lapse that we celebrate takes only one and a half days, from 3 p.m. on Friday to dawn on Sunday.

Years ago, a friend, dearer to me than my own life, moved away. It was sudden, unexpected, and caused me to grieve more than if he had died, I think. For those of mine who had died still seemed a part of me somehow. A few weeks after his departure I was sitting in my living room engrossed in a book. A knock at the door interrupted my reading. I "heard" it, Mary. But I was not startled. I simply sat there and "heard" the door open, "heard" footsteps in the entryway. I did not turn my head; I experienced no curiosity, no fear, simply a sense of expectation and welcome. I "felt" his entry into the room, his coming up behind me and around the curve of the couch and knew his sitting down beside me. That was all; yet that was everything. We sat there together for a few moments, a couple of minutes, an hour. I do not remember for I was unaware of any passage of time. My friend who left, who continues to live thousands of miles away, returned to me and remains with me to this day. It is a mystery which touched me, one that I have never sought to tamper with or take apart. In the whole acceptance of it, I am changed.

In microcosm, that barest nudge of small mystery leads me to imagine you awakening on the "third day" into a fullness of spirit you have never felt before. As you get up and dress, you marvel at this new feeling and pause several times to send mental fingers within yourself softly touching, testing all the tender pain places you had taken to bed with you the night before. You push harder at your psyche, dare the unbearable, and see again Jesus on that criminal's cross. But, wonder of wonders, no gasp of grief grabs at your throat, no surge of hurting engulfs your heart, no crushing sorrow uncoils within you. Instead, an incredible sense of beauty bathes this most terrible of scenes. Light the color of extraordinary love enfolds you, holds you transfixed so that you cannot break silence even to greet Yahweh in whose presence you know you now stand more profoundly than ever before. You do not think, you do not question, you do not seek to understand, only to absorb this most dynamic, most active burst of life you have ever experienced. It is a moment out of time, beyond imagining and seems to have always been.

A babble of voices flutters into your consciousness, hands, arms, bodies press against you, a confusion of movement and clamor. "Mary, he's alive! Mary, oh Mary, Jesus has risen. . . alive. . . talked to us. . . tomb empty. . . alive . . . real like me. . . risen. . . tell the others. . . he said to tell. . . this morning. . . dawn. . . Jesus is risen! Let's tell the others. . . we wanted you to know first, Mary. He is risen from the dead, Mary. You'll see him. Risen!''

The commotion disappears out the door as quickly as it had intruded, leaving your room crowded with the vibrations of their excited sounds and feelings. ''But I already knew,'' you whisper. ''In that eternal moment I knew my son risen, transformed of body, breathing, breaking bread, eating. My own son and yet more than my son, talking, teaching, corporal yet passing through doors, unrecognized yet known, walking to Emmaus and frying fish on the shores of Galilee. I knew him already ascended, returned to you, Yahweh, yet remaining always with us, with all of us unto the last generation. I feel his transforming spirit, the spirit he promised us all, more part of me than ever his tiny body growing within my womb was. Ah, Yahweh, once I asked you 'How can this be?' this mysterious impregnation of my body. But now, Yahweh, I do not ask how, this even more mysterious impregnation of my soul. Not now do I ask. Not ever. I am newly alive with our son, Yahweh, with you.''

And so, on this third day without end, am I newly alive with you, Mary, with all my sisters and brothers and, yes, lizards and birds, grasses and flowers, alive in Christ, your son, Jesus, transformed in resurrection, embracing us all.

Sharing the
Gift of Healing

Awaking reluctantly this morning, the sun finally shrugged off the clouds and lazed its way across the sky to listlessly lay itself down in the west. Now a cooling breeze has come out of hiding and perked up the entire neighborhood with its gentle touch. Would that I could perform the same grace for some people in whose troubled lives I have been involved these past few weeks. But then maybe, unlike the breeze which will be gone by midnight, I wish for myself a role which is not mine to play. I wish for a magic wand, a magic potion, a magic word which will touch these friends of mine and cause them to perk up with the realization that the power of healing is within themselves already, that it is a process which, at this point, they need only activate in order to make themselves whole.

From one person I accepted the burden of interacting with her brother who was spiraling into clinical depression. She felt herself being adversely affected by his behavior and unable to give him the listening time

he needed. I saw him through to his eventual hospital-
ization and release and promise to continue needed
medication and psychiatric counseling. The third person is their mother, fragile with age and unspoken,
even unrecognized, anxieties and fears, who has accepted a certain level of expressed depression in her life
as the norm, unwittingly distancing herself from those
from whom she wants, and needs, the most emotional
support. To them all I have been listener, nurturer,
counselor, helper. But like the breeze, I, too, have my
midnight and it is time now to begin the withdrawal
process that will allow me to shed those roles and become, again, friend. All three have experienced a resurrection of one sort or another and must now live out
their fifty days to their own pentecosts.

I've thought often about that rented room in Jerusalem. Remember it, Mary? The one upstairs? Remember
the evening when you and members of your family,
along with a few close friends, had gathered there as
you so often did these days? You had read some scripture, recited some psalms, shared the prayer that Jesus
had taught the apostles. Now the others were wondering aloud where the eleven (once twelve) were but you
remained silent, sensing the reason for their absence.
And then, a short time later, when the tread of their
footsteps sounds on the stairs, you go to the door and
open it.

Peter, the first to enter, embraces you, then steps
back a bit. "He has gone," he says quietly. You nod in
acknowledgement of what you already knew and move
aside to let the other men enter. Each greets you in his
own way, a bear hug from one, a lingering touch from
another, a caressing hold from still another. John, the
last to enter, grabs you fiercely, wordlessly, then leads
you to a cushion where you both sit, he clinging to your
hand, while the others mingle with those assembled,

telling them your son's final directives to his followers. The message, though spoken as if new, and listened to in the same manner, is really not new. "Stay in Jerusalem. . . you will be baptized in the spirit. . . the holy spirit. . . wait. . . you will witness to the ends of the earth." Ever since his resurrection Jesus had been saying those words. And in his very saying of them they had come to pass. "But they do not know. How long," you wonder, "until they discern that the reality is in the very promise." Beside you, John, now relaxed, seems lost in his own thoughts. Seeing the others begin to form into a prayer circle, you tug him out of his reverie and both of you join with them. The room feels hot and airless until you close your eyes and slip into the cool depths of Yahweh within yourself.

Those first few days pass in a flurry. There are things to do: arrangements to be made, sleeping room to be found, meals to be planned, food to be bought. Any hour of the day or night brings another one, two or seven more disciples of Jesus to join in the vigil formed to await the coming of the holy spirit. Peter, ever mindful of scripture, calls for an election of one to take the place of Judas Iscariot. After careful and prayerful consideration, Matthias, is chosen.

By this time there are about 120 believers present and a certain routine has been established. Peter does a surprisingly good job of organizing and directing the large group. But it is you who are called upon to soothe a young woman, encourage a disciple beginning to doubt, tease a morose young man into laughter, cajole an older woman into more considerate cooperation. You feel the excitement in them all, some more than others, and know it is only a matter of time before the winds of the spirit stir their imaginations into recognition and acceptance of the strength and power which will enable them to actively participate in the building of the kingdom your son spoke of. And it begins. Just a stirring. First in Peter, then Mary of Magdala. In John and Thomas, Martha and Bartholomew. The stirring becomes a breeze wafting about all the rest and you feel the contagion pass through the room like a strong wind, a wondrous wind, a playful, joy-filled wind. Surprise, wonder, exhilaration, the freedom of passionate conviction takes them all by storm. The power that will enable each and every one of them to live life, to preach and teach life, to enlarge and deepen life, is finally upon them, let loose from the stillpoint within them.

Tears of exultation shine in your eyes as you open your arms to those nearest you. But only for a moment. Preparations to leave this upper room are already in progress. The time to fan out among peoples everywhere has come. The time to lay the foundation for the kingdom is at hand. Though the days ahead will bring measures of frustration, of anger, of rivalries, of depression, the joy of this empowerment, of this newly recognized knowledge of ''being able to'' will run like a river throughout your lives and in Jesus' name you will all do great things.

As will my three friends, Mary, and friends everywhere, if they remain in their own upper rooms, in their own interior places long enough to catch the first faint rustlings of spirit within them.

A New Time of Waiting

The sun got up this morning and played hide-and-seek with the clouds before giving up and leaving them to gloom up all the landscape in sight. I snuggled in bed for awhile to ward off the chill waiting to wrap itself around my joints the minute I got up. But further sleep escaped me. I could feel my body stiffening from lying there too long so I rose, turned up the heat, dressed and let the cat out. She was back in five minutes and we breakfasted together. Then, while attending to the few chores necessary in keeping house for me and the cat, an old love appeared from the recesses of my memory and kept me company. This happens more and more these days. Those whose lives deeply intersected mine return in spirit as comfortable companions.

This afternoon I took a nap and woke to a drizzling rain. Since dinner I've been working on a jigsaw puzzle from which I am sure an edge piece is missing. While sifting through the shapes, I've been trying to ignore the aches and pains that the dampness seems to inten-

sify. We do get older, Mary. Depending on our basic
personalities, we rant and rave or complain and sniffle
or gracefully bend into it. In any case, we have no
choice.

I've been thinking about you tonight, wondering if
you, too, rationalized your short-term lapses of memory while living easily with crystal clear images of years
past; whether you found sleep elusive at night yet nodded off comfortably during the day. And did the summer sun seem not so hot anymore while winter's chill
just got colder and colder?

In the years since Jesus' final parting in Galilee,
you've given your time and energy to your son's mission. Though the gospels tell us he spoke the words to
his 11 chosen friends only, telling them to ''go into the
whole world and proclaim the gospel to every crea-
ture,'' you and the other women accept his commis-
sioning as well and become activists in spreading the
good news. You work to feed the hungry, clothe the naked, give shelter to the homeless, comfort the sorrow-
ing and help the afflicted. You manage quietly to preach
and to teach.

Indeed, since the apostles took seriously their task
to preach to the whole world they were often absent
and the responsibility of maintaining and strengthen-
ing those base churches fell to you and the other
women. Without your combined efforts those churches
might never have survived into the next generation.

But now you have returned to Nazareth, to your
own home which you share with old Clove, the velvety,
brownish cat who, lean and hungry, attached herself to
you when you were last in Bethany. Now she is fat and
glossy and has adapted herself to your routine. Your
only quarrel with her is when guests appear, as they do
with some frequency. Then she raises her back, spits
spitefully and trounces off to the sleeping alcove, never

appearing until the last person has left. A courteous cat she is not!

You spend most days quietly, reflectively. A house empty of children needs surprisingly little upkeep. You do a little gardening, very little, because the knees and the back do not take well to it anymore. Besides, the days when you needed large amounts of food on hand have long since disappeared. In fact, if it weren't for Clovie's insatiable appetite for cinnamon-flavored yogurt you might forget to eat sometimes. But she never fails to remind you that a meal ought to be served.

Every evening while you are clearing the dishes, old Clovie climbs up into the chair near the door and curls herself into a furry ball and snoozes, one forepaw always extended beyond the chair, spoiling the round symmetry of the rest of her body. And every evening, when you are through, you walk over to the chair, push her off, and settle into the warmth her body has left on the seat. Old Clovie tosses her head, mews an epithet, goes out the door, then turns right around and comes back to leap up and settle, purring, into your lap.

This is a special time for you, one you look forward to throughout the day. This is when you talk with Joseph, your beloved Joseph with whom you shared so much. After the ritual scratching behind her ears, the cat raises her head and watches you intently, waiting for the conversation to begin. Once it does, she eavesdrops shamelessly, occasionally putting in a mewing word of her own.

There are others you speak with, of course: Yahweh, always Yahweh; your mother; your son, too; so many whose spirits still crowd your little house. With most, it's just a passing greeting born of a warm memory. But Joseph is different. With him you are forever young no matter your aging. With him you shared the miracle of Jesus' birth. With him you shared the waiting—waiting for your son's birth, waiting to return from Egypt, waiting for Jesus' first step, first word, first day of school, recovery from sickness. But most of all, with him you shared yourself, body and soul, in the deepest intimacy of human love.

Now a new time of waiting has come to you. Somehow it seems comfortable and right that you should share this one with Joseph too. "Soon, my beloved, I will be joining you. I don't know when exactly but I sense it will not be too long. And then we will be together forever. You and me and our Jesus."

Old Clovie stirs in your lap, nudging you affectionately. She may not understand the import of your words but she senses the receptive and joyful waiting of your mood and dozes off content that great things are in store for you, as they are for all of us who remain constant in love, pregnant with faith and hope.

The Pulse
of the Earth

Winter's storms have spent their passions and moved on leaving our land green and pregnant, crowned with crocuses and freesias, daffodils and hyacinths. And I, midwife to my backyard plot of ground, touch the earth gently and wonder at this newest genesis of creation.

In the dirt, my fingers feeling through the leafy mulch to the damp soil beneath, I suddenly sense a pulse, a heartbeat that matches my own, and yours, and all who have ever bloomed on this planet; all of us, and nature herself, caught up in communion with the strongest heartbeat of all, that of your son, risen and alive. The music is suddenly all around and within me as if the entire universe were singing and I know the arms of Yahweh enfolding me.

The hours have passed since I experienced that tiny inbreaking of the kingdom that Jesus spoke of so often, but the hum of it lingers on, energizing the spirit that still wants to dance no matter the creaky old bones

barely containing it. So I sit here in the waning lavender
light of day and play freezetag with my memories,
waltzing through my mind to touch the young idealistic
girl I was, the one who looked on you with such awe
and wanted so to emulate the lovely goddess figure you
had been turned into. And there, I catch myself married, pregnant, determined to be the maiden madonna
that I thought you were. And over there, in the
shadows, the young woman coping with husband and
knee-deep in children and parish involvement and cub
scouts and wondering how I could ever have thought
you, ''perfect mother with your perfect child,'' capable
of being my friend. A swift turn and I tag myself, a tan-
gle of grief, anger, betrayal, pain. My husband is gone
and I am alone with the children and no one to right the
injustice of it all. Not even God. And still it never occurred to me that you might understand.

Oh Mary, so many years were to pass until I grew
up enough to begin thinking about the woman locked
inside all those plaster and plastic images of you. Look!
Right there, under that rising grin of a moon. Quick!
Tag them! You and me, two women, both of us
stretched tall in laughter. Not tinkling-cymbal sounding, pious-prattle pealing sorts of self-applause but ex-
ultant fullbodied, soul-resonating magnificats, each of
us according to our own capacities. Look at us, two old
women, tears twinkling like stars on our cheeks as our
joy bubbles up in that laughter that shimmers in the
night. For we survived it all. The misunderstandings
and accusations, the manipulations and oppressions,
the poverties of relationships and goods, all the obsta-
cles that our worlds, hundreds of years apart, placed in
front of us. Admittedly, you did it sooner and better
than I. But Mary, where would I have been if you had
not been so graciously there, waiting for me to break
through my own defenses, through the socializations

that had imprisoned me, waiting for me to accept the
gift of my own mind and intuition so that I might turn to
you in imagination and tentatively talk to you, dialogue
with you, empathize with you and finally know you not
as an idealized version of spiritual femininity but as a
fully alive human woman whose walk through life paralleled so many of my own paths.

Come sit with me now, beloved sister, mother of
my Lord. Clasp my hand and let us rejoice in each other's company, celebrating our vindication as women.
Let us share quietly the realities of our lives, the deaths
and disappointments, the healings and the hap-
pinesses, the growing up of children to their own integ-
rities, the final letting go of them, the reclaiming of ourselves as persons. Let us talk about all the experiences
that unfolded within us a confidence and a competence
to cooperate with God in creating an environment in
which his kingdom need not be briefly episodic but
whole and entire and lasting.

Tradition has it that you were assumed, body and
soul, into heaven. I am certain of the truth contained in
that statement: that body and soul are inextricably in-
tertwined; that Yahweh created this world and found it
good; that he created us all and found us good; that
though we flawed his creation by sin he still found us so
good that he chose one of us to conceive and bear his
son, trusted you to raise him to manhood so that he
might suffer the death-dealing effects of sin and tri-
umph over them. In his resurrection is our life. In his
humanity is our divinity.

Thank you, Mary.